The Complete Guide to Growing Roses: From Red to Black

Copyright Page

TITLE: The Complete Guide to Growing Roses of All Colors: From Red to Black

1ST Edition

ISBN: 9798223912484

Table of Contents

The Complete Guide to Growing Roses of All Colors: From Red to Black

By Roberto Miguel Rodriguez

Chapter 1: Introduction to Growing Roses

The Beauty and Charm of Roses

Roses have long been celebrated as the epitome of beauty and charm in the world of flowers. Their vibrant colors, delicate petals, and intoxicating fragrance make them a favorite among gardeners and flower enthusiasts alike. In this subchapter, we will delve into the captivating world of roses, exploring the different colors and varieties available and providing valuable tips and techniques for growing and nurturing these magnificent blooms.

One of the most sought-after varieties of roses is the black rose. Although black roses do not naturally occur in nature, there are several dark-colored varieties that can create the illusion of blackness. We will guide you on how to grow these enigmatic beauties, including tips for selecting the right variety, soil preparation, and proper care to ensure their dark hues remain vibrant and intense.

Red roses, often associated with love and passion, are another classic choice for any garden. We will provide you with expert advice on how to grow red roses, including the best cultivars to choose from, ideal growing conditions, and essential care tips to ensure the blossoms are radiant and abundant.

White roses, symbolizing purity and innocence, exude elegance and grace. We will share valuable insights on growing white roses, including tips for maintaining their pristine color, preventing disease, and enhancing their delicate fragrance.

Pink roses, available in a spectrum of shades, are a popular choice for their romantic allure. We will explore the various hues of pink roses and offer guidance on cultivating them successfully, from selecting the right variety to pruning techniques that promote abundant blooms.

Yellow roses, with their vibrant and sunny hues, bring warmth and cheerfulness to any garden. We will provide you with techniques for growing yellow roses that boast intense and vibrant colors, as well as tips for maintaining their health and vigor.

Purple roses, often associated with enchantment and mystery, add a touch of magic to any garden. We will share expert advice on growing purple roses, including tips for enhancing their color, preventing discoloration, and creating a captivating display of purple hues.

Blue roses, though rare in nature, are highly sought after for their unique and ethereal beauty. We will guide you on nurturing blue roses successfully, discussing the various methods used to achieve their captivating color and offering tips for maintaining their vibrancy.

If you seek a garden bursting with an array of colors, we will provide you with insights on growing multi-colored roses. From bi-colored blooms to those with intricate patterns, we will explore the techniques and strategies for cultivating these stunning varieties.

For those with a taste for the rare and exotic, we will offer tips on cultivating unique rose varieties that will truly make your garden stand out. From striped roses to those with unusual shapes and fragrances, we will guide you through the process of selecting, planting, and caring for these extraordinary blooms.

Lastly, we will provide special care instructions for black roses and other dark-colored varieties. These roses require specific attention to maintain their deep and intense hues, and we will share the best practices to ensure their longevity and beauty.

Whether you are a seasoned gardener or just starting your rose-growing journey, this subchapter will equip you with the knowledge and techniques to grow roses of all colors, from the passionate reds to the mysterious blues. Get ready to create a rose garden that will mesmerize and delight all who behold its beauty.

The Importance of Choosing the Right Rose Varieties

In the world of gardening, roses are often regarded as the epitome of beauty, elegance, and sophistication. With their vibrant colors and captivating fragrances, these flowers have the power to transform any garden into a stunning oasis. However, choosing the right rose varieties is of utmost importance to ensure a successful and visually appealing rose garden. In this subchapter, we will explore the significance of selecting the appropriate rose varieties for different color preferences and the specific care required for each.

Whether you are aiming for a garden bursting with red roses, dreaming of delicate white blooms, or yearning for the elusive black rose, understanding the characteristics of each variety is crucial. Each color carries its own symbolism and aesthetic appeal, making it essential to choose roses that not only match your personal preferences but also complement the overall design of your garden.

For those seeking the classic allure of red roses, selecting a variety known for its rich color and strong fragrance is essential. Varieties such as 'Mr. Lincoln' and 'Mister Lincoln' are renowned for their deep crimson petals and intoxicating scent, making them perfect choices for romantic gardens or bouquets.

On the other hand, cultivating white roses requires careful attention to detail. Varieties like 'Iceberg' or 'Pope John Paul II' exhibit pristine white blooms that symbolize purity and innocence. To maintain their pristine appearance, gardeners should ensure proper sunlight exposure and regular pruning.

Pink roses offer a wide range of shades, from soft pastels to vibrant fuchsias. Varieties like 'Cecile Brunner' or 'Eden Rose' are popular choices, providing an array of pink hues to suit any garden design. Regular deadheading and adequate watering are crucial to maintaining their vibrant colors.

For those desiring the sunny cheerfulness of yellow roses, varieties like 'Graham Thomas' or 'Julia Child' are excellent options. These roses boast vibrant hues that can brighten up any garden space. Adequate sunlight exposure and well-drained soil are key factors in successfully cultivating yellow roses.

Purple roses, such as 'Ebb Tide' or 'Midnight Blue,' exude an air of mystery and grace. These rare and exotic varieties require specific care, including regular fertilization and protection from extreme temperatures.

The enigma of blue roses has captivated gardeners for centuries. Although truly blue roses are yet to be naturally bred, varieties like 'Blue Moon' or 'Rhapsody in Blue' offer the closest approximation. These roses require diligent care, including soil acidification and proper watering techniques.

For those seeking a mixture of colors, multi-colored roses like 'Joseph's Coat' or 'Seduction' provide a stunning display of various shades within a single bloom. These unique varieties add a touch of whimsy and charm to any garden.

Lastly, special care must be taken when cultivating black roses or other dark-colored varieties. Ensuring adequate sunlight exposure, proper pruning, and soil fertility are essential to maintain their dramatic beauty.

In conclusion, choosing the right rose varieties is crucial in creating a vibrant and visually appealing rose garden. By understanding the specific care requirements for each color preference, gardeners can ensure their roses thrive and provide a stunning display of nature's beauty. Whether it's the allure of red, the purity of white, the charm of pink, the cheerfulness of yellow, the elegance of purple, the enigma of blue, the whimsy of multi-colored varieties, or the dramatic beauty of black roses, selecting the appropriate varieties is the key to a successful and diverse rose garden.

Understanding the Basics of Rose Cultivation

Roses are one of the most popular and beloved flowers among gardeners around the world. Their beauty, fragrance, and endless variety of colors make them a delightful addition to any garden. However, growing roses can seem like a daunting task, especially if you are new to gardening or have never cultivated this particular flower before. This subchapter aims to provide you with a comprehensive understanding of the basics of rose cultivation, ensuring that you can successfully grow roses of all colors, including the elusive black roses.

To begin your journey into rose cultivation, it is important to understand the different varieties and their specific needs. Red roses, for example, thrive in full sunlight and well-drained soil. They require regular watering and benefit from regular pruning to promote healthy growth. White roses, on the other hand, prefer slightly acidic soil and partial shade. They are more prone to diseases, so regular monitoring and care are necessary.

Pink roses come in various shades, from soft blush to vibrant fuchsia. They generally prefer full sun and well-drained soil. Yellow roses, known for their vibrant hues, require ample sunlight and fertile soil. They are relatively easy to grow and are resistant to diseases.

Purple roses are a symbol of enchantment and mystery. They need well-drained soil and moderate sunlight to thrive. Blue roses, although rare and difficult to cultivate, can be grown by carefully manipulating their genetic makeup. They require acidic soil and consistent care.

If you are interested in growing multi-colored roses, you can achieve this by grafting different rose varieties onto the same rootstock. This technique allows you to create stunning combinations of colors and patterns in your garden.

Rare and exotic rose varieties require special care and attention. They often have specific soil and climate requirements. It is essential to research and understand the unique needs of these varieties to ensure their successful cultivation.

For those aspiring to create a rose garden with a diverse range of colors, it is crucial to plan the layout carefully. Consider the height, growth habits, and color combinations of different rose varieties to create a visually pleasing and harmonious display.

Finally, black roses and other dark-colored varieties require special care due to their sensitivity to sunlight. Plant them in partial shade and provide regular watering to prevent the leaves from scorching.

By understanding the basics of rose cultivation, you can confidently embark on your journey to grow roses of all colors, including the elusive black roses. With proper care, attention, and a little bit of patience, you will be rewarded with a beautiful garden filled with the enchanting beauty and fragrance of roses.

Essential Tools and Equipment for Growing Roses

Growing roses of all colors, including rare and exotic varieties, requires careful planning and the right tools and equipment. To ensure successful cultivation and to create a vibrant and diverse rose garden, gardeners need to be equipped with the following essential tools:

1. Pruning Shears: Pruning is an essential part of rose care, and having a good pair of pruning shears is crucial. Look for shears with a bypass design, as they provide clean cuts and minimize damage to the rose bushes.

2. Garden Gloves: Protect your hands from thorns and potential irritants in the soil by wearing sturdy garden gloves. Choose gloves that fit well and offer good dexterity to make handling roses easier.

3. Trowel: A trowel is a handy tool for digging holes and transplanting roses. Look for a trowel with a comfortable handle and a sturdy blade that can withstand the pressure of digging in dense soil.

4. Garden Fork: A garden fork is useful for loosening compacted soil and improving drainage around rose bushes. It also helps in aerating the soil, allowing the roots to breathe and absorb nutrients more effectively.

5. Watering Can or Hose: Roses require regular watering, especially during dry spells. Invest in a reliable watering can or hose with a nozzle attachment for precise and gentle watering.

6. Fertilizer: To promote healthy growth and vibrant blooms, roses need regular feeding. Choose a balanced rose fertilizer that contains essential nutrients like nitrogen, phosphorus, and potassium. Follow the instructions on the packaging for proper application.

7. Mulch: Mulching around rose bushes helps retain moisture, suppresses weed growth, and regulates soil temperature. Organic mulches like shredded leaves or bark chips are ideal for roses.

8. Plant Supports: Depending on the variety, some roses may require support to prevent them from drooping or being damaged by strong

winds. Bamboo stakes or trellises can provide the necessary support while adding aesthetic value to the garden.

9. pH Testing Kit: Roses prefer slightly acidic soil with a pH range of 6 to 6.5. Test the soil regularly using a pH testing kit to ensure it is within the optimal range. Adjustments can be made by adding lime to raise pH or sulfur to lower it.

10. Pest and Disease Control: Roses are susceptible to various pests and diseases. Keep a range of organic pest control products, such as insecticidal soap and neem oil, handy to combat common pests like aphids and fungal diseases like black spot.

By arming yourself with these essential tools and equipment, you will be well-prepared to grow roses of all colors, including rare and exotic varieties. Remember to maintain regular care, provide proper nutrition and water, and create an environment that encourages healthy growth. With the right tools and a little patience, your rose garden will flourish with a stunning array of colors, from red to black and everything in between.

Chapter 2: How to Grow Roses of All Colors, Including Black Roses

The Fascination Behind Black Roses

Black roses have long been shrouded in mystery and intrigue, captivating the imagination of gardeners and rose enthusiasts alike. With their dark, velvety petals and enigmatic beauty, these flowers have a unique allure that sets them apart from their vibrant counterparts. In this subchapter, we will delve into the fascination behind black roses, exploring their origins, symbolism, and the techniques required to successfully grow and care for these captivating blooms.

Black roses, although not naturally occurring, have been cultivated over the years through hybridization and selective breeding. Their deep, almost black hue is not a result of pigment, but rather a dark red or purple shade that creates the illusion of blackness. This rarity and uniqueness contribute to their appeal, making them highly sought after by gardeners looking to add a touch of mystique to their gardens.

Symbolically, black roses have been associated with various meanings throughout history. While often associated with death and mourning, they can also represent rebirth, transcendence, and the unknown. Their dark beauty has inspired countless poets, artists, and writers, who have used them as a metaphor for love, passion, and the mysteries of life.

Growing black roses requires special attention and care. These roses thrive in well-drained soil with ample sunlight, but they are also more sensitive to extreme temperatures and require protection from frost. Proper pruning techniques and regular fertilization are essential to encourage healthy growth and abundant blooms. Additionally, black roses benefit from a balanced pH level and regular watering, ensuring their roots remain hydrated without becoming waterlogged.

To maintain the intensity of their color, black roses require some additional care. They are prone to fading under prolonged exposure to sunlight, so providing them with shade during the hottest parts of the day is recommended. Deadheading spent blooms and removing any diseased or damaged foliage will also help promote new growth and maintain the overall health and appearance of the plant.

In conclusion, black roses hold a unique fascination for gardeners, offering a touch of mystery and elegance to any garden. With their deep, velvety petals and symbolic significance, these blooms are sure to captivate the imagination. By following the proper techniques and providing the necessary care, gardeners can successfully cultivate and enjoy the beauty of black roses, creating a stunning and diverse display in their gardens.

Selecting the Best Black Rose Varieties

Subchapter: Selecting the Best Black Rose Varieties

Black roses have captivated gardeners and flower enthusiasts for centuries, with their mysterious and alluring beauty. While true black roses do not exist naturally, there are several varieties that come close to achieving this enchanting hue. In this subchapter, we will explore the different black rose varieties available and provide tips for selecting the best ones for your garden.

When it comes to black roses, it's important to note that the term "black" refers to the deep, dark red or purple color that these roses exhibit. One popular variety is the 'Black Baccara,' which features velvety petals that appear almost black in certain lighting conditions. Another option is the 'Black Magic,' a hybrid tea rose with deep burgundy blooms that exude elegance and sophistication.

For those seeking a more unusual black rose variety, consider the 'Black Jade.' This miniature rose produces clusters of deep maroon flowers, making it a stunning addition to any garden or floral arrangement. Similarly, the 'Black Ice' rose boasts a striking blackish-red color and a strong fragrance, making it a favorite among rose enthusiasts.

When selecting black rose varieties, it is essential to consider factors such as disease resistance, growth habit, and fragrance. Look for roses that have strong disease resistance to ensure they thrive in your garden. Additionally, consider the growth habit of the rose, as some varieties may be more suitable for containers or smaller spaces, while others work well as climbers or shrubs.

Fragrance is another crucial aspect to consider when choosing black rose varieties. Some black roses, like the 'Black Baccara,' emit a delightful scent that adds to their overall appeal. However, others may not have a strong fragrance, so it's important to determine your preference beforehand.

Lastly, when cultivating black roses, provide them with the special care they require. These dark-colored varieties tend to benefit from regular pruning, ample sunlight, and well-draining soil. Consider mulching around the base of the plants to conserve moisture and prevent weed growth.

In conclusion, selecting the best black rose varieties for your garden involves considering factors such as disease resistance, growth habit, fragrance, and special care requirements. By choosing the right black roses, you can create a garden that exudes elegance and intrigue.

Preparing the Soil for Black Roses

Black roses are often seen as mysterious and unique, captivating the hearts of gardeners and flower enthusiasts alike. While they may not exist naturally in nature, creating the perfect conditions for these dark beauties to thrive is not as daunting as it may seem. Preparing the soil is a crucial step in ensuring the successful growth of black roses, as it provides the necessary nutrients and structure for the plants to flourish. In this subchapter, we will explore the specific requirements for cultivating black roses and how to prepare the soil to meet those needs.

Black roses, like any other rose variety, require well-drained soil that is rich in organic matter. Start by choosing a location that receives at least six hours of direct sunlight each day, as this is essential for their growth. It is also important to ensure that the soil pH is slightly acidic, ranging from 5.5 to 6.5. Test your soil using a pH testing kit, and if necessary, make adjustments by adding organic materials such as compost or peat moss.

Before planting your black roses, it is crucial to prepare the soil by removing any weeds, rocks, or debris. This will provide a clean and healthy environment for your plants to establish their roots. Loosen the soil to a depth of about 12 inches, breaking up any clumps and ensuring a loose and friable texture.

To boost the fertility of the soil, incorporate well-rotted compost or aged manure. These organic amendments will enhance the soil structure, improve drainage, and provide the necessary nutrients for your black roses to thrive. Spread a layer of compost or manure over the planting area, about 2 to 3 inches thick, and work it into the soil using a garden fork or tiller.

Once the soil is prepared, it is time to plant your black roses. Dig a hole that is wide and deep enough to accommodate the root ball of the plant, ensuring that the bud union (the swollen part where the rose was grafted onto the rootstock) is level with or slightly above the soil surface. Backfill the hole with the amended soil, gently firming it around the roots.

Remember to water your newly planted black roses thoroughly and regularly, especially during dry spells. Mulching around the plants with organic materials like wood chips or straw will help retain moisture and suppress weeds.

With proper soil preparation and care, you can create the ideal growing conditions for black roses to flourish. The dark and enigmatic blooms will add an intriguing touch to your garden, captivating all who behold their beauty.

Planting and Caring for Black Roses

Black roses have always held a mysterious allure, captivating gardeners with their dark and velvety petals. While they may not be truly black in color, they can range from deep burgundy to a rich, dark red or purple. If you're a gardener looking to add these enchanting beauties to your collection, here's a guide on how to plant and care for black roses.

Choosing the Right Variety:

When selecting black roses, it's important to know that there is no true black rose variety. The shades of black are achieved through hybridization to enhance the depth of color. Look for varieties such as Black Baccara, Black Magic, or Midnight Blue for the closest approximation of black roses.

Planting:

Black roses require the same basic planting conditions as other rose varieties. Choose a well-draining location with at least six hours of direct sunlight. Prepare the soil by incorporating organic matter and ensuring a pH level between 6.0 and 6.5. Dig a hole deep enough to accommodate the roots and gently place the rose plant, making sure the bud union is at or slightly above ground level. Fill the hole with soil, firming it gently around the roots.

Watering and Fertilizing:

Black roses have similar watering needs to other rose varieties. They prefer regular, deep watering rather than shallow and frequent irrigation. Water the plants at the base, avoiding wetting the foliage to prevent diseases. During the growing season, fertilize your black roses every four to six weeks with a balanced rose fertilizer to promote healthy growth and abundant blooms.

Pruning and Maintenance:

Regular pruning is essential for black roses to maintain their shape and encourage new growth. Prune in early spring, removing dead or damaged wood, as well as any crossed or crowded branches. Aim to keep the plant open and airy, allowing sunlight and air circulation to reach all parts of the plant. Mulching around the base of the roses will help conserve moisture, suppress weeds, and regulate soil temperature.

Protection and Care:

Black roses can be more susceptible to diseases such as black spot and powdery mildew due to their darker foliage. Regularly inspect your plants for signs of disease or pests and take appropriate action. Additionally, during periods of extreme heat or cold, provide extra protection by shading the plants or covering them to prevent damage.

Black roses are truly unique and can add a touch of drama and elegance to any garden. By following these planting and care guidelines, you'll be well on your way to growing these captivating dark beauties and enjoying their enchanting presence in your garden.

Pruning and Training Techniques for Black Roses

Black roses are incredibly alluring and mysterious, adding a touch of drama and elegance to any garden. However, cultivating and caring for these dark beauties requires special attention. In this subchapter, we will explore the pruning and training techniques specifically tailored for black roses, ensuring their optimal growth and stunning display.

Pruning is an essential step in maintaining the health and shape of black roses. It promotes new growth, enhances air circulation, and prevents diseases. The best time to prune black roses is in early spring, just as new growth begins. Start by removing any dead or damaged wood, cutting it back to healthy tissue. Next, eliminate any crossing or rubbing branches to prevent future issues. To encourage bushier growth, prune back one-third of the total height of the rose, cutting just above an outward-facing bud.

Training black roses requires careful consideration, as their dark color tends to absorb more heat than other varieties. Choose a location that receives at least six hours of direct sunlight daily, ensuring the roses have enough warmth to thrive. Additionally, provide a sturdy support structure, such as a trellis or stake, to prevent the heavy blooms from bending or snapping the stems.

Regular maintenance is crucial for black roses. Water deeply and consistently, ensuring the soil remains moist but not waterlogged. Mulching around the base of the plants will help retain moisture and suppress weed growth. Fertilize regularly with a balanced rose fertilizer, following the manufacturer's instructions. Remember that black roses tend to be heavy feeders, so a nutrient-rich soil is essential for their optimal growth.

Black roses are prone to diseases such as black spot and powdery mildew. To prevent these issues, ensure proper air circulation around the plants by spacing them adequately. Regularly remove any fallen leaves or debris from the base of the rose to eliminate potential breeding grounds for pests and diseases. If necessary, use organic fungicides or insecticides to treat any infestations promptly.

In conclusion, black roses are a captivating addition to any garden, but they require specific pruning and training techniques for their successful growth. By following the guidelines outlined in this subchapter, gardeners can cultivate healthy black roses that will enchant and mesmerize with their dark allure.

Chapter 3: How to Grow Red Roses

The Symbolism and Passion of Red Roses

Red roses have long been associated with love, passion, and romance. They are the ultimate symbol of true affection and are often given to express deep emotions. In this subchapter, we will explore the significance of red roses and provide valuable tips on how to grow them successfully.

Red roses have a rich and storied history, dating back centuries. They have been depicted in art, literature, and poetry as a representation of love and desire. Their vibrant color and velvety petals make them a captivating addition to any garden or bouquet.

When it comes to growing red roses, there are a few key factors to consider. First and foremost, selecting the right variety is crucial. Look for roses that are known for their intense red color and strong fragrance. Some popular choices include 'Red Velvet,' 'Ingrid Bergman,' and 'Mister Lincoln.' These varieties are not only beautiful but also relatively easy to grow.

To ensure the health and vitality of your red roses, proper care is essential. They thrive in well-drained soil and require at least six hours of direct sunlight each day. Regular watering and fertilizing will help promote healthy growth and abundant blooms. Pruning is also important to maintain the shape and appearance of your rose bushes.

In addition to their symbolic meaning, red roses also make a stunning addition to mixed-color rose gardens. Pair them with white roses for a classic and elegant look, or combine them with pink roses to create a romantic and feminine display. For a more dramatic effect, consider planting red roses alongside purple or yellow varieties.

Lastly, it's worth noting that black roses, while not truly black, are a unique and intriguing addition to any garden. These deep red roses have dark, velvety petals that create a striking contrast. They require special care and attention, including regular fertilizing and protection from extreme temperatures.

In conclusion, red roses hold a special place in the hearts of gardeners and flower enthusiasts. Their symbolism and passion make them a beloved choice for expressing deep emotions. Whether you're a novice gardener or a seasoned rose enthusiast, growing red roses can be a rewarding and fulfilling experience. With the right care and attention, these vibrant blooms will bring beauty and joy to your garden for years to come.

Choosing the Perfect Red Rose Varieties

When it comes to growing roses, there is a wide array of colors to choose from. However, nothing quite captures the essence of romance and passion like a red rose. With their vibrant and bold hues, red roses are a classic choice for any garden. In this subchapter, we will explore the different varieties of red roses and how to choose the perfect one for your garden.

Firstly, it's important to understand that red roses come in various shades, each with its unique charm. From deep velvety reds to bright and fiery hues, there is a red rose variety to suit every gardener's preference. Some popular red rose varieties include 'Mr. Lincoln,' 'Red Eden,' 'Black Baccara,' and 'Chrysler Imperial.'

When selecting a red rose variety, consider factors such as fragrance, disease resistance, and growth habit. For those seeking a fragrant red rose, 'Double Delight' and 'Don Juan' are excellent choices. If disease resistance is a priority, 'Knock Out' and 'Mister Lincoln' are known for their resilience. Additionally, consider the growth habit of the rose variety – whether it is a bush, climber, or hybrid tea – and ensure it aligns with your garden's design and space availability.

Furthermore, it's crucial to consider the climate and growing conditions in your area. Some red rose varieties thrive in specific climates, while others are more adaptable. Research the growing requirements of each variety to ensure it will flourish in your garden. Factors such as sunlight exposure, soil pH, and watering needs should also be taken into account.

Lastly, don't be afraid to mix and match different red rose varieties to create a visually stunning and diverse garden. Pairing deep red roses with lighter shades of pink or white can create a beautiful contrast. Alternatively, combine red roses with other colors, such as yellow or purple, to create a vibrant and lively display.

In conclusion, choosing the perfect red rose varieties is an exciting endeavor for any gardener. Consider factors such as fragrance, disease resistance, growth habit, and climate suitability when selecting the ideal red rose variety for your garden. By carefully choosing and combining different red rose varieties, you can create a captivating and enchanting display of color in your garden.

Soil Preparation for Red Roses

Growing red roses requires careful attention to soil preparation. The quality of the soil plays a vital role in the overall health and vigor of your red rose plants. In this subchapter, we will discuss some essential tips and techniques for preparing the soil to ensure your red roses thrive and bloom beautifully.

First and foremost, it is crucial to choose the right location for your red roses. They prefer a spot that receives at least 6 hours of direct sunlight daily. Once you have identified the ideal location, it's time to prepare the soil.

Start by clearing the area of any weeds or grass. This will help prevent competition for nutrients and water. Next, loosen the soil using a garden fork or tiller. This will improve drainage and aeration, allowing the roots to penetrate easily.

Red roses thrive in well-draining soil with a slightly acidic pH level ranging from 6.0 to 6.5. Conduct a soil test to determine the pH level and make any necessary adjustments. If the soil is too alkaline, you can lower the pH by adding organic matter such as compost or well-rotted manure. On the other hand, if the soil is too acidic, you can add lime to raise the pH level.

To improve the fertility of the soil, incorporate organic matter like compost or aged manure. This will enhance the nutrient content and water-holding capacity of the soil. Ensure that the organic matter is well-rotted to prevent any potential damage to the roots.

Before planting your red roses, it is advisable to mix in a slow-release rose fertilizer. This will provide the necessary nutrients for the plants to establish strong roots and encourage vibrant blooms.

Once the soil preparation is complete, dig a hole large enough to accommodate the root ball of the rose plant. Place the rose in the hole, ensuring that the bud union is level with the soil surface. Backfill the hole with the amended soil, gently firming it around the roots.

After planting, water the roses thoroughly to settle the soil around the roots. Mulching around the base of the plants will help conserve moisture, suppress weeds, and regulate soil temperature.

Remember to monitor the moisture levels regularly and water as needed, ensuring the soil remains evenly moist but not waterlogged.

By following these guidelines for soil preparation, your red roses will have the best possible start, resulting in healthy plants and stunning blooms that will bring joy to any garden.

Planting and Nurturing Red Roses

Red roses are perhaps the most iconic and timeless flowers in the world of gardening. Their vibrant hue and intoxicating fragrance have captivated gardeners for centuries. If you're looking to add a touch of romance and elegance to your garden, red roses are the perfect choice. In this subchapter, we will explore the art of planting and nurturing red roses, ensuring that they thrive and bloom to their full potential.

When it comes to planting red roses, the first step is selecting the right variety for your climate and soil conditions. There are numerous types of red roses available, each with its own growth habits and care requirements. Hybrid teas, climbers, and shrub roses are some popular options to consider. Consult a local nursery or gardening expert to determine which varieties are best suited for your region.

Before planting, it is crucial to prepare the soil properly. Red roses prefer well-drained soil enriched with organic matter. Amend the soil with compost or well-rotted manure to improve its fertility and drainage. Choose a sunny location for your roses, as they require at least six hours of direct sunlight daily.

Once the soil is prepared, dig a hole large enough to accommodate the rose's root ball. Place the rose in the hole, ensuring that the bud union is level with or slightly above the soil surface. Backfill the hole with soil, firming it gently around the roots. Water thoroughly to settle the soil and eliminate any air pockets.

Proper watering is essential for the health and vitality of red roses. While they require regular watering, it is important not to overwater, as this can lead to root rot. Aim for a deep watering once or twice a week, providing around one inch of water. Mulching around the base of the plant can help retain moisture and suppress weeds.

To promote vigorous growth and abundant blooms, it is crucial to feed red roses regularly. Apply a balanced rose fertilizer in early spring, following the manufacturer's instructions. Repeat the application every six weeks throughout the growing season. Additionally, supplement with organic matter, such as compost or aged manure, to enrich the soil and provide essential nutrients.

Pruning is another vital aspect of red rose care. Prune in early spring, removing any dead, damaged, or crossing branches. Shape the plant to encourage an open, airy growth habit and improve air circulation. Regular pruning will stimulate new growth and promote the production of more vibrant blooms.

In conclusion, planting and nurturing red roses requires careful attention to detail and adherence to proper care practices. By selecting the right variety, preparing the soil adequately, providing ample sunlight and water, feeding regularly, and pruning effectively, you can cultivate red roses that will grace your garden with their beauty and fragrance for years to come.

Pruning and Maintaining Red Roses

Red roses are a classic symbol of love and passion, and they are a popular choice for many gardeners. To keep your red roses healthy and thriving, proper pruning and maintenance are essential. In this subchapter, we will discuss the best practices for pruning and maintaining red roses to ensure beautiful blooms year after year.

Pruning is an essential step in the care of red roses. It helps stimulate new growth, remove dead or diseased wood, and shape the plant for optimal growth. The best time to prune your red roses is in early spring, just before new growth begins. Start by removing any dead or damaged wood, cutting it back to healthy green wood. Next, prune any crossing branches or those that are growing inward towards the center of the plant. This will help improve airflow and reduce the risk of diseases. Finally, shape the plant by trimming the remaining branches to create a balanced and aesthetically pleasing form.

In addition to pruning, regular maintenance is crucial for the health of your red roses. Watering is an essential aspect of rose care, especially during dry spells. Provide your red roses with deep watering at least once a week, ensuring that the water reaches the roots. Mulching around the base of the plants can help retain moisture and suppress weeds.

Fertilizing is another important aspect of maintaining red roses. Apply a balanced rose fertilizer in early spring and again in mid-summer to provide the necessary nutrients for healthy growth and abundant blooms. Be sure to follow the manufacturer's instructions on the fertilizer package for the correct application rates.

Pest and disease control is also vital for maintaining red roses. Keep an eye out for common rose pests such as aphids, thrips, and black spot. Regularly inspect your plants and take appropriate measures, such as using organic pesticides or insecticidal soaps, to control these nuisances.

Finally, proper winter protection is crucial for red roses, especially in colder regions. Before the first frost, mulch around the base of the plants to insulate the roots and protect them from freezing temperatures. Additionally, consider covering the plants with burlap or a rose cone to shield them from harsh winter winds.

By following these pruning and maintenance tips, you can ensure that your red roses remain healthy, vibrant, and full of blooms. Whether you are a seasoned gardener or just starting out, these practices will help you cultivate beautiful red roses that will be the envy of your garden.

Chapter 4: Tips for Growing White Roses

The Timeless Elegance of White Roses

White roses have long been praised for their timeless elegance and purity, making them a favorite among gardeners and rose enthusiasts. In this subchapter, we will explore the beauty of white roses, their symbolism, and provide you with expert tips on how to grow and care for these delicate blooms.

White roses are often associated with innocence, purity, and new beginnings. Their pristine petals evoke a sense of tranquility and grace, making them a popular choice for weddings, anniversaries, and other special occasions. Whether you choose to grow them as standalone plants or incorporate them into a diverse rose garden, white roses are sure to add a touch of sophistication and elegance to any landscape.

When it comes to growing white roses, there are a few key tips to keep in mind. Firstly, it is essential to select a suitable variety for your climate and soil conditions. White roses, like other rose varieties, thrive in well-draining soil with a pH level between 6.0 and 6.5. Ensure that your chosen location receives at least six hours of direct sunlight daily to promote healthy growth and abundant blooms.

Regular watering is crucial for white roses, especially during the hot summer months. Aim for deep, infrequent watering to encourage the development of deep roots. Mulching around the base of the plants can help retain moisture and suppress weeds.

Pruning is another essential aspect of caring for white roses. Regular pruning promotes air circulation, reduces the risk of disease, and encourages vigorous growth. In early spring, remove any dead, damaged, or crossing branches. Prune the remaining stems to maintain an open, vase-like shape.

To keep your white roses looking their best, it is essential to address common pests and diseases. Regularly inspect your plants for aphids, spider mites, and powdery mildew. If you notice any signs of infestation or disease, promptly treat your roses with organic insecticides or fungicides.

In conclusion, white roses epitomize elegance and purity, making them a timeless addition to any garden. By following our expert tips on growing and caring for white roses, you can create a stunning display of these delicate blooms that will captivate and inspire all who see them.

Selecting the Best White Rose Varieties

White roses are a classic choice for any garden, adding an elegant and timeless beauty to the landscape. Whether you're a seasoned gardener or just starting out, growing white roses can be a rewarding experience. In this subchapter, we will guide you through the process of selecting the best white rose varieties for your garden.

When choosing white rose varieties, there are a few factors to consider. First, you'll want to think about the size and shape of the rose bush. Some white roses are compact and bushy, making them ideal for smaller gardens or containers. Others are climbers, perfect for covering trellises or fences. Determine the space you have available and select a variety that fits your needs.

Next, consider the bloom size and shape. White roses come in a range of petal formations, from tightly packed blooms to more loosely arranged flowers. Take into account your personal preference and the overall aesthetic you want to achieve in your garden.

Another important consideration is fragrance. Many white rose varieties have a delightful scent, which can enhance the enjoyment of your garden. If fragrance is important to you, look for varieties known for their strong and pleasant scents.

It's also essential to select white rose varieties that are disease-resistant. Roses are susceptible to various diseases, such as blackspot and powdery mildew. Choosing disease-resistant varieties will save you time and effort in maintaining the health of your plants.

Some popular white rose varieties to consider include 'Iceberg,' 'Madame Hardy,' 'White Licorice,' and 'Polar Ice.' These varieties are known for their beautiful blooms, fragrance, and disease resistance. However, there are many other white rose varieties available, so don't hesitate to explore and discover unique options that suit your taste.

In conclusion, selecting the best white rose varieties for your garden involves considering factors such as size, shape, fragrance, and disease resistance. By choosing the right varieties, you can create a stunning and enchanting white rose garden that will be the envy of all gardeners. Happy gardening!

Soil Preparation for White Roses

White roses are timeless and elegant, adding a touch of grace to any garden. To ensure the health and vibrancy of your white roses, it is essential to prepare the soil properly. In this subchapter, we will guide you through the process of soil preparation specifically tailored for white roses.

White roses thrive in well-drained soil that is rich in organic matter. Begin by selecting a location in your garden that receives at least six hours of direct sunlight daily. Once you have chosen the perfect spot, it's time to prepare the soil.

First, remove any weeds or grass from the area. This will prevent them from competing with your white roses for nutrients and water. Next, loosen the soil using a garden fork or tiller. This will improve the soil's aeration and drainage, allowing the roots to grow deep and strong.

To enhance the fertility of the soil, incorporate organic matter such as compost or well-rotted manure. Spread a layer of about two to three inches evenly over the area and mix it into the soil using a garden rake. Organic matter not only provides essential nutrients but also improves the soil's ability to retain moisture.

Before planting your white roses, it is crucial to ensure the soil's pH level is suitable. White roses prefer slightly acidic soil with a pH range of 6.0 to 6.5. You can easily test the pH level using a soil testing kit available at garden centers. If the pH level is too high, add sulfur or peat moss to lower it. Conversely, if the pH level is too low, add lime to raise it.

Once the soil is prepared, it is time to plant your white roses. Dig a hole that is slightly wider and deeper than the root ball of the rose plant. Gently place the rose plant into the hole, ensuring that the bud union is level with or slightly above the soil surface. Backfill the hole with the soil mixture, firming it gently around the roots.

Remember to water your white roses thoroughly after planting, and provide them with regular watering throughout the growing season. By following these soil preparation techniques, you will create the perfect foundation for your white roses to flourish and showcase their beauty in your garden.

Planting and Caring for White Roses

White roses are classic and elegant, adding a touch of serenity and purity to any garden. Whether you are a seasoned gardener or just starting out, growing white roses can be a rewarding experience. In this subchapter, we will explore the steps to successfully plant and care for white roses, ensuring they thrive and bloom beautifully in your garden.

When it comes to planting white roses, it's important to choose the right location. These roses prefer full sun, so find a spot in your garden that receives at least six hours of direct sunlight each day. Additionally, make sure the soil is well-draining and rich in organic matter. Before planting, amend the soil with compost or well-rotted manure to provide the roses with the nutrients they need.

To plant white roses, dig a hole that is wide and deep enough to accommodate the root ball. Gently remove the rose from its container, being careful not to damage the roots. Place the rose in the hole, making sure it sits at the same level as it did in the container. Backfill the hole with soil, firming it gently around the roots. Water the newly planted rose thoroughly to settle the soil.

Caring for white roses involves regular watering, especially during dry spells. Aim to keep the soil evenly moist, but not waterlogged. Mulching around the base of the rose will help retain moisture and suppress weeds. Additionally, feeding your white roses with a balanced rose fertilizer in early spring and mid-summer will promote healthy growth and abundant blooms.

Pruning white roses is essential to maintain their shape and encourage new growth. Prune in late winter or early spring, removing any dead or diseased wood and cutting back any crossing or overcrowded branches. This will improve air circulation and reduce the risk of diseases.

To keep your white roses looking their best, be vigilant for pests and diseases. Common problems include aphids, blackspot, and powdery mildew. Regularly inspect your roses and take appropriate action if you spot any issues. Using organic pest control methods and proper sanitation practices will help keep your roses healthy.

In conclusion, growing white roses requires some attention and care, but the results are truly worth it. By selecting the right location, planting correctly, and providing proper care, you can enjoy the beauty and elegance of white roses in your garden. So go ahead and add these enchanting blooms to your collection, and watch as they transform your garden into a serene haven of white.

Pruning and Training Techniques for White Roses

White roses are a classic and elegant addition to any garden. Their pure and pristine blooms symbolize purity, innocence, and new beginnings. To ensure your white roses thrive and produce abundant blooms, it is essential to understand the proper pruning and training techniques.

Pruning is a vital aspect of rose care that promotes healthy growth and abundant flowering. The best time to prune white roses is in early spring, just before new growth emerges. Start by removing any dead, damaged, or diseased wood, cutting it back to healthy tissue. This helps prevent the spread of disease and encourages new growth.

Next, look for any crossing or rubbing branches and remove them to allow for better air circulation and light penetration. This helps prevent fungal diseases and encourages the development of strong, healthy stems. Additionally, thin out any overcrowded areas to promote better airflow and reduce the risk of pests and diseases.

When it comes to training white roses, it is essential to provide support and structure for their sprawling growth habit. This is especially important for climbing or rambling varieties. Install trellises, arbors, or stakes to guide the growth of your white roses and prevent them from sprawling on the ground.

Regularly tie the rose canes to the support structure using soft garden twine or stretchy ties, ensuring they are not too tight to allow for natural movement and growth. As your white roses grow, carefully weave the canes through the support structure to encourage a tidy and well-trained appearance.

It is also crucial to regularly deadhead your white roses throughout the growing season. Removing spent blooms not only keeps the plant looking tidy but also encourages the production of new flowers. Make clean cuts just above a set of healthy leaves or an outward-facing bud to promote healthy growth.

Lastly, don't forget to feed your white roses regularly. Use a balanced rose fertilizer or organic compost to provide the necessary nutrients for vigorous growth and abundant flowering. Follow the manufacturer's instructions for application rates and frequencies.

By following these pruning and training techniques, you will ensure that your white roses remain healthy, vigorous, and produce an abundance of beautiful blooms. Remember to always observe and respond to the specific needs of your white roses, as individual varieties may have unique requirements. With proper care and attention, your white roses will be the highlight of your garden, adding a touch of elegance and beauty.

Chapter 5: Growing Pink Roses in Different Shades

The Delicate Beauty of Pink Roses

Pink roses are a quintessential symbol of grace, elegance, and romance in the world of flowers. Their delicate beauty and soft hues make them a favorite among gardeners and rose enthusiasts. In this subchapter, we will explore the various shades of pink roses and provide valuable tips on how to grow them successfully in your garden.

Pink roses come in a spectrum of shades, ranging from pale blush to vibrant fuchsia. Each shade carries its own unique charm and can add a touch of femininity and serenity to any garden. When selecting pink rose varieties, consider factors such as bloom size, fragrance, and disease resistance to ensure a thriving and visually stunning display.

To grow pink roses, start by selecting a suitable location in your garden that receives at least six hours of direct sunlight each day. Roses thrive in well-drained soil, so amend the planting area with organic matter and ensure proper drainage. It is advisable to plant pink roses in early spring or late fall when the weather is cool.

When it comes to watering, pink roses prefer consistent moisture but not overly wet conditions. Water deeply and regularly, especially during dry spells, and avoid wetting the leaves to prevent diseases such as powdery mildew. Mulching around the base of the plants will help retain moisture and suppress weed growth.

Pruning is essential for maintaining the health and shape of your pink roses. In early spring, remove any dead or damaged wood and prune to shape the plants. Regularly deadhead spent blooms to encourage continuous flowering throughout the season. This will also prevent the formation of rose hips, redirecting energy back into the plant.

Pink roses are generally hardy, but they can still be susceptible to common rose diseases such as black spot and aphid infestations. Regularly inspect your plants for signs of disease or pests, and promptly treat any issues with appropriate organic or chemical remedies.

In conclusion, pink roses are a delightful addition to any garden, bringing a touch of elegance and charm. By following the tips and techniques outlined in this subchapter, you can successfully cultivate pink roses in various shades and create a stunning display of delicate beauty in your garden. Whether you prefer soft pastels or vibrant pinks, these roses are sure to captivate and enchant both you and your visitors.

Exploring Various Shades of Pink Roses

Pink roses are known for their delicate beauty and romantic symbolism. They come in a wide range of shades, each with its own unique charm. In this subchapter, we will delve into the world of pink roses and explore the different shades that can be cultivated in your garden.

Light Pink Roses:

Light pink roses are often associated with grace, elegance, and femininity. They create a soft and romantic atmosphere in any garden. Varieties such as 'Fairy Tale' and 'Pink Simplicity' are popular choices for their dainty blooms and subtle fragrance. These roses thrive in well-drained soil and require regular watering.

Medium Pink Roses:

Medium pink roses are slightly more vibrant than their lighter counterparts. They add a touch of vibrancy and energy to your garden.

'Beverly' and 'Queen Elizabeth' are popular medium pink rose varieties that are easy to grow and maintain. These roses prefer full sun and well-drained soil.

Dark Pink Roses:

Dark pink roses, also known as hot pink or magenta roses, are bold and eye-catching. They make a striking statement in any garden. Varieties such as 'Pink Panther' and 'Hot Cocoa' are known for their intense color and strong fragrance. These roses require regular pruning and fertilization to thrive.

Blush Pink Roses:

Blush pink roses have a subtle and delicate hue that resembles the color of a blush on one's cheeks. They exude a sense of innocence and purity. Varieties like 'Blush Noisette' and 'Wedding Bells' are cherished for their ethereal beauty and sweet fragrance. These roses thrive in well-drained soil and partial shade.

Coral Pink Roses:

Coral pink roses have a warm and vibrant tone that adds a tropical touch to any garden. They are often associated with enthusiasm and excitement. Varieties such as 'Coral Cove' and 'Coral Drift' are highly sought after for their unique color and disease resistance. These roses require regular watering and protection from extreme temperatures.

In this subchapter, we have explored the various shades of pink roses, from light and delicate to bold and vibrant. By incorporating these beautiful roses into your garden, you can create a romantic and enchanting space that will captivate your senses. Whether you prefer the softness of light pink or the boldness of dark pink, there is a shade of pink rose that will suit your tastes. With proper care and attention, these roses will flourish and bring joy to your garden for years to come.

Soil Preparation for Pink Roses

Pink roses are a classic and beloved addition to any garden. Their delicate and romantic blooms come in a variety of shades, from soft blush to vibrant fuchsia. To ensure the health and success of your pink roses, proper soil preparation is essential. This subchapter will guide you through the steps necessary to create the optimal growing conditions for your pink roses.

First and foremost, it is crucial to choose the right location for your pink roses. They thrive in full sun, so select a spot in your garden that receives at least six hours of direct sunlight each day. Once you have found the perfect spot, it's time to prepare the soil.

Start by removing any weeds or grass from the area. Pink roses prefer well-draining soil, so it's important to improve the drainage if necessary. If your soil tends to retain water, consider incorporating organic matter such as compost or well-rotted manure. This will help to loosen the soil and improve its structure.

Next, test the pH level of your soil. Pink roses generally prefer slightly acidic soil with a pH between 6.0 and 6.5. If your soil is too alkaline, you can lower the pH by adding sulfur or peat moss. On the other hand, if your soil is too acidic, you can raise the pH by adding lime.

After adjusting the pH, it's time to enrich the soil with nutrients. Pink roses benefit from a balanced fertilizer, such as a 10-10-10 or 14-14-14 formula. Apply the fertilizer according to the package instructions, being careful not to overdo it. Too much fertilizer can burn the roots of your roses.

Finally, it's essential to properly prepare the planting hole for your pink roses. Dig a hole that is wide and deep enough to accommodate the root ball of the rose bush. Gently loosen the roots and place the rose bush in the hole, making sure that the bud union (the swollen area where the rose was grafted onto the rootstock) is level with or slightly above the soil surface. Backfill the hole with soil, firming it gently around the roots.

By following these soil preparation guidelines, you will provide your pink roses with the optimal growing conditions they need to thrive. With proper care and attention, you can enjoy a stunning display of pink blooms in your garden year after year.

Planting and Nurturing Pink Roses

Subchapter: Planting and Nurturing Pink Roses

Pink roses are undoubtedly one of the most beloved and popular choices among gardeners. Their delicate and romantic blooms can add a touch of elegance to any garden. In this subchapter, we will explore the various aspects of planting and nurturing pink roses, including different shades and techniques for successful cultivation.

When it comes to planting pink roses, selecting the right location is crucial. Pink roses thrive in well-drained soil that receives at least six hours of direct sunlight each day. Prepare the soil by incorporating organic matter such as compost or aged manure to provide essential nutrients and improve drainage.

Before planting, soak the rose bush in water for a few hours to hydrate the roots. Dig a hole that is wide and deep enough to accommodate the roots without crowding. Place the rose bush in the hole, making sure the bud union (the swollen area where the rose was grafted onto the rootstock) is at ground level. Backfill the hole with soil, firming it gently to remove any air pockets.

Nurturing pink roses requires regular watering, especially during the hot summer months. Water deeply at the base of the plant to encourage the roots to grow deeper. Mulching around the rose bush helps retain moisture and suppresses weeds. Prune the roses in late winter or early spring to remove dead or diseased wood and promote healthy growth.

Pink roses come in a range of shades, from soft pastels to vibrant hot pinks. To achieve the desired shade, it is essential to choose the right rose variety. Some popular pink rose varieties include 'Queen Elizabeth,' 'Peace,' 'Ballerina,' and 'Pink Parfait.' Consider the size, fragrance, and disease resistance of the roses when selecting the varieties for your garden.

To enhance the beauty of your pink rose garden, consider companion planting with other flowers that complement the pink blooms. Some excellent options include lavender, salvia, catmint, and baby's breath. This combination not only adds visual interest but also attracts beneficial insects to your garden.

In conclusion, planting and nurturing pink roses can be a rewarding experience for any gardener. With the right selection of varieties, proper planting techniques, and regular care, you can create a stunning display of pink roses in your garden. Remember to provide adequate water, sunlight, and nutrients to ensure healthy growth and vibrant blooms. Happy gardening!

Pruning and Maintaining Pink Roses

Pink roses are a popular choice among gardeners due to their delicate beauty and romantic symbolism. Whether you are a seasoned rose grower or a beginner looking to add a touch of elegance to your garden, this subchapter will guide you through the essential steps for pruning and maintaining pink roses.

Pruning is a crucial aspect of rose care that helps promote healthy growth, prevent diseases, and encourage abundant blooms. It is best to prune pink roses during early spring when the dormant period is ending. Start by removing any dead, damaged, or diseased canes with a clean and sharp pair of pruning shears. Then, trim the remaining canes to about 1/3 of their original height, making clean cuts just above an outward-facing bud.

Regular maintenance is equally important to ensure the vitality of your pink roses throughout the growing season. Watering is vital, especially during dry periods, so be sure to provide deep soakings rather than shallow watering. Mulching around the base of the roses helps retain moisture and suppress weed growth. Additionally, applying a slow-release fertilizer in early spring and again in midsummer will provide the necessary nutrients for healthy growth.

To keep your pink roses looking their best, regular deadheading is essential. This involves removing spent blooms by cutting just above a healthy bud or a five-leaflet leaf. Deadheading not only improves the appearance of the plant but also encourages new blooms to form.

When it comes to pest and disease management, prevention is key. Regularly inspect your pink roses for signs of aphids, black spot, or powdery mildew. If detected, treat them promptly with organic insecticides or fungicides to prevent further damage.

Lastly, providing adequate support for climbing or rambling pink rose varieties is vital. Install trellises, arches, or stakes to guide the growth and prevent the canes from sprawling on the ground.

By following these pruning and maintenance tips for pink roses, you will be rewarded with a stunning display of vibrant and fragrant blooms. Remember, each rose variety may have specific care requirements, so it is essential to consult the instructions provided by the breeder or nursery. With dedication and proper care, your pink roses will thrive and become the centerpiece of your garden, delighting both your eyes and your senses.

Chapter 6: Cultivating Yellow Roses with Vibrant Hues

The Bright and Sunny Appeal of Yellow Roses

Yellow roses have a special place in the hearts of gardeners for their bright and sunny appeal. These radiant blooms bring a splash of warmth and cheerfulness to any garden, making them a popular choice among rose enthusiasts. In this subchapter, we will delve into the world of yellow roses and explore the techniques and tips for cultivating these vibrant beauties.

Yellow roses come in a wide range of hues, from pale lemon to deep golden tones. Their vibrant colors are perfect for adding a pop of brightness to any garden setting. Whether you are looking to create a stunning focal point or enhance your existing flower beds, yellow roses are a fantastic choice.

When it comes to growing yellow roses, it is important to choose the right variety and provide the proper care. Start by selecting a rose variety that is known for its vibrant yellow color and disease resistance. Some popular yellow rose varieties include 'Golden Celebration,' 'Julia Child,' and 'Midas Touch.' These varieties are not only beautiful but also relatively easy to grow.

To ensure the healthy growth of your yellow roses, provide them with adequate sunlight and well-drained soil. Yellow roses thrive in full sun, so make sure to choose a location in your garden that receives at least six hours of direct sunlight each day. Additionally, yellow roses prefer soil that is rich in organic matter and drains well. Amend the soil with compost or well-rotted manure before planting to improve its texture and fertility.

Regular watering is essential for the optimal growth of yellow roses. Water deeply and thoroughly, making sure to soak the soil around the roots. However, be cautious not to overwater, as this can lead to root rot. Mulching around the base of the plants can help retain moisture and suppress weed growth.

Yellow roses, like other rose varieties, benefit from regular fertilization. Apply a balanced rose fertilizer in early spring and again in mid-summer to promote healthy growth and abundant blooms. Pruning is also crucial for maintaining the shape and vigor of your yellow roses. Prune in late winter or early spring, removing any dead or damaged wood and shaping the bushes as desired.

With proper care and attention, your yellow roses will reward you with a stunning display of bright and sunny blooms. Their vibrant colors will bring joy and beauty to your garden, creating a captivating sight for all to admire. So, whether you are a seasoned gardener or a beginner, don't miss out on the opportunity to cultivate these delightful yellow roses and enjoy the splendor they bring to your outdoor space.

Selecting the Best Yellow Rose Varieties

Yellow roses are a symbol of friendship, joy, and happiness. Their vibrant hues can add a cheerful touch to any garden or flower arrangement. However, with so many yellow rose varieties to choose from, it can be overwhelming to select the best ones for your garden. In this subchapter, we will guide you through the process of selecting the best yellow rose varieties that will thrive in your garden.

When selecting yellow rose varieties, it is important to consider factors such as growth habit, disease resistance, and fragrance. Some popular yellow rose varieties that meet these criteria include 'Midas Touch,' 'Julia Child,' and 'Sunny Sky.'

'Midas Touch' is a compact rose that produces large, golden yellow blooms. This variety is known for its disease resistance and strong fragrance, making it a favorite among many gardeners. 'Julia Child' is another excellent choice, with its buttery yellow blooms and strong licorice fragrance. This variety is also highly disease resistant and can tolerate a wide range of climates.

For those looking for a climbing yellow rose variety, 'Sunny Sky' is a great option. This variety produces clusters of bright yellow blooms and has a moderate fragrance. It is also disease resistant and can grow up to 10 feet tall, making it a stunning addition to any garden trellis or fence.

Aside from these popular varieties, there are also lesser-known yellow rose varieties that are worth considering. 'Graham Thomas' is a classic English rose with large, cup-shaped flowers and a strong tea fragrance. 'Golden Celebration' is another standout variety, with its rich, golden yellow blooms and fruity fragrance.

When selecting yellow rose varieties, it is important to choose ones that suit your garden's specific needs and conditions. Consider factors such as climate, soil type, and available sunlight. Additionally, pay attention to the specific care requirements of each variety, as some may require more attention and maintenance than others.

In conclusion, selecting the best yellow rose varieties for your garden can be an exciting and rewarding process. By considering factors such as growth habit, disease resistance, and fragrance, you can choose varieties that will thrive in your garden and bring joy to your gardening experience. Whether you prefer compact roses, climbing varieties, or unique blooms, there is a perfect yellow rose variety out there for you. Happy gardening!

Soil Preparation for Yellow Roses

Yellow roses are a stunning addition to any garden, bringing warmth and brightness to the landscape. To ensure that your yellow roses thrive and produce vibrant blooms, proper soil preparation is essential. In this subchapter, we will explore the necessary steps to prepare the soil for growing yellow roses.

1. Soil pH: Yellow roses prefer slightly acidic soil with a pH level between 6.0 and 6.5. Test the soil using a pH testing kit, and if necessary, adjust the pH by adding lime or sulfur accordingly. This will create the ideal growing environment for your yellow roses.

2. Organic Matter: Incorporating organic matter into the soil is crucial for optimum growth. Add well-rotted compost, aged manure, or peat moss to improve soil structure, drainage, and fertility. This will provide the necessary nutrients for your yellow roses to flourish.

3. Drainage: Yellow roses thrive in well-draining soil. Ensure that your planting area has proper drainage by amending heavy clay or compacted soil with sand or perlite. This will prevent waterlogging, which can lead to root rot and other diseases.

4. Nutrients: Yellow roses require a balanced supply of nutrients to promote healthy growth and abundant blooms. Prior to planting, enrich the soil with a slow-release rose fertilizer or organic amendments such as bone meal, blood meal, or fish emulsion. Follow the manufacturer's instructions for proper application rates.

5. Mulching: Apply a layer of organic mulch around the base of your yellow roses to help retain moisture, regulate soil temperature, and suppress weed growth. Use materials like bark chips, straw, or compost. Avoid placing mulch directly against the stems to prevent rot and diseases.

6. Soil Moisture: Yellow roses appreciate consistent soil moisture, but they also dislike wet feet. Water deeply and thoroughly, allowing the

soil to dry slightly between watering sessions. Use a soaker hose or drip irrigation system to ensure even water distribution.

By following these soil preparation tips, you will provide your yellow roses with the perfect growing conditions. Remember to monitor the soil's moisture levels, regularly inspect for pests or diseases, and provide adequate sunlight for optimal growth. With proper care, your yellow roses will reward you with their vibrant hues and enchanting fragrance, enhancing the beauty of your garden.

Planting and Caring for Yellow Roses

Yellow roses are a beautiful addition to any garden, adding a vibrant pop of color that can brighten up even the dullest of spaces. Whether you're a seasoned gardener or just starting out, learning how to plant and care for yellow roses is a must. In this subchapter, we will explore the techniques and tips that will help you cultivate healthy and vibrant yellow roses.

To begin, it is essential to choose the right variety of yellow rose for your garden. There are numerous options available, ranging from pale pastels to vibrant and bold hues. Consider the overall aesthetic of your garden and the colors that will complement the existing flora.

When it comes to planting yellow roses, selecting the right location is crucial. Yellow roses thrive in full sunlight, so choose a spot that receives at least six hours of direct sunlight each day. Additionally, ensure that the soil is well-draining, as yellow roses prefer soil that is rich and loamy.

Before planting your yellow rose, prepare the soil by incorporating organic matter, such as compost or well-rotted manure. This will provide essential nutrients and improve the overall health of the plant. Dig a hole that is wide and deep enough to accommodate the root ball, ensuring that the bud union is level with or slightly above the soil surface.

Once your yellow rose is planted, regular watering is essential, especially during the initial establishment period. Water deeply, ensuring that the root zone is thoroughly saturated. Be mindful not to overwater, as this can lead to root rot. A layer of mulch around the base of the plant will help retain moisture and deter weeds.

Fertilizing your yellow rose is also necessary to promote healthy growth and abundant blooms. Apply a balanced rose fertilizer in early spring, following the manufacturer's instructions. Repeat the application every six weeks throughout the growing season.

Pruning is another essential aspect of caring for yellow roses. In late winter or early spring, remove any dead or damaged wood, as well as any crossing or congested branches. This will help improve airflow and prevent disease.

Lastly, be vigilant for common rose diseases, such as blackspot and powdery mildew. Regularly inspect your yellow roses for any signs of disease or pests and take immediate action if necessary. There are numerous organic and chemical treatments available to help combat these issues.

In conclusion, cultivating vibrant and healthy yellow roses requires careful consideration of variety, proper planting techniques, regular watering, fertilizing, and pruning. With the right care and attention, your yellow roses will thrive, adding a burst of sunshine and beauty to your garden.

Pruning and Training Techniques for Yellow Roses

Yellow roses are a beautiful addition to any garden, adding a touch of sunshine and warmth. However, to ensure their optimal growth and vibrant color, it is essential to employ proper pruning and training techniques. In this subchapter, we will explore the various methods to nurture and care for yellow roses, enabling gardeners to achieve the best results.

Pruning yellow roses is crucial for their health and appearance. It is recommended to prune them in early spring, just before new growth begins. Start by removing any dead, damaged, or diseased branches, making clean cuts at a 45-degree angle. This will promote air circulation and prevent the spread of diseases. Additionally, thin out any crowded areas to allow sunlight to reach the center of the plant.

Training yellow roses to grow in a desired shape can enhance their overall beauty. One popular technique is called "pegging." This involves bending the canes of the rose bush and securing them to the ground using garden stakes or wire. By doing so, more energy is directed towards lateral bud growth, resulting in a bushier and more abundant display of blooms.

To encourage the growth of vibrant yellow hues, it is essential to provide the roses with proper nutrition. Fertilize regularly with a balanced rose fertilizer, rich in nitrogen, phosphorus, and potassium. Additionally, supplement the soil with organic matter, such as compost or well-rotted manure, to improve its fertility and drainage.

Watering yellow roses adequately is crucial for their overall health. They prefer deep, infrequent watering rather than frequent shallow watering. Aim to water at the base of the plant, avoiding wetting the foliage to prevent the development of fungal diseases. Mulching around the base of the rose bush will help retain moisture and control weed growth.

Lastly, protect yellow roses from pests and diseases. Regularly inspect the plants for any signs of aphids, spider mites, or black spot. Treat infestations promptly with appropriate organic or chemical controls to prevent further damage.

By employing these pruning and training techniques, gardeners can successfully cultivate vibrant yellow roses in their gardens. Remember to adapt these techniques to the specific needs and requirements of the rose variety being grown. With proper care and attention, yellow roses will flourish and bring joy to any garden.

Chapter 7: Techniques for Growing Purple Roses

The Mysterious and Enchanting World of Purple Roses

As gardeners, we are constantly seeking new and exciting varieties of roses to add beauty and intrigue to our gardens. And what could be more intriguing than the mysterious and enchanting world of purple roses? These captivating blooms are sure to add a touch of magic to any landscape.

Purple roses are not only visually stunning, but they also hold a special symbolism. Often associated with enchantment and mystery, purple roses are the perfect choice for those looking to create a sense of intrigue in their garden. Whether you're a seasoned gardener or just starting out, growing purple roses can be a rewarding and fulfilling experience.

When it comes to growing purple roses, there are a few key techniques to keep in mind. First and foremost, it's important to choose the right variety. There are many different shades of purple, from deep, dark hues to lighter lavender tones. Consider your garden's overall color scheme and choose a shade that will complement your existing plants.

Purple roses thrive in well-drained soil with plenty of organic matter. Make sure to amend your soil with compost or aged manure before planting. This will provide the necessary nutrients for healthy growth and vibrant blooms.

Proper pruning is also essential for growing purple roses. Regular pruning will help maintain the shape and size of the plant, as well as encourage new growth and flowering. Be sure to remove any dead or diseased wood, as this can hinder the overall health of the plant.

In addition to proper care and maintenance, it's important to give your purple roses the special attention they deserve. These unique blooms require a little extra care to reach their full potential. Regular watering, especially during dry periods, is crucial to keep the plants hydrated and thriving. Additionally, a layer of mulch around the base of the plant will help retain moisture and suppress weeds.

With their captivating beauty and mysterious allure, purple roses are a must-have for any garden enthusiast. Their unique color adds a touch of magic to any landscape and creates a sense of enchantment that is truly captivating. So why not dive into the world of purple roses and create your own magical garden oasis? With a little care and attention, you can enjoy these enchanting blooms for years to come.

Exploring Different Shades of Purple Roses

Purple roses are a captivating addition to any garden, bringing a touch of elegance and mystique. With their rich hues and velvety petals, they are sure to make a statement. In this subchapter, we will delve into the world of purple roses, exploring the different shades and techniques for growing these enchanting flowers.

Purple roses come in a wide spectrum of shades, ranging from soft lavender to deep plum. Each shade evokes a different mood and can be used to create various effects in your garden. For a romantic and whimsical feel, consider planting pale lavender roses. These delicate blooms are perfect for creating a dreamy atmosphere in your outdoor space. On the other hand, if you prefer a more dramatic look, opt for deep purple roses. These bold flowers will add a sense of mystery and intrigue to your garden.

When it comes to growing purple roses, there are a few key techniques to keep in mind. First and foremost, it is important to choose the right variety for your climate and soil conditions. Some purple roses are more tolerant of colder temperatures, while others thrive in warmer climates. Additionally, ensure that your roses receive ample sunlight and are planted in well-draining soil. Regular watering and fertilizing will also help your purple roses flourish.

Nurturing blue roses successfully is another topic of interest for gardeners. While true blue roses do not exist in nature, there are varieties that display shades of blue or lavender. These roses can be a stunning addition to your garden, but they require special care. Blue roses prefer acidic soil, so consider amending your soil with sulfur to achieve the desired pH level. Additionally, regular pruning and deadheading will help promote healthy growth and vibrant blooms.

Cultivating multi-colored roses is another exciting avenue to explore. By grafting different rose varieties together, you can create stunning blooms that showcase a range of colors. This technique allows you to experiment with different combinations and create truly unique flowers.

In conclusion, growing purple roses offers a world of possibilities for gardeners. Whether you prefer soft lavender or deep plum, these enchanting flowers are sure to add beauty and charm to your garden. By following the proper techniques and care tips, you can successfully cultivate a diverse range of purple roses and create a truly stunning display in your outdoor space.

Soil Preparation for Purple Roses

When it comes to cultivating purple roses, proper soil preparation is essential to ensure their healthy growth and vibrant color. In this subchapter, we will guide you through the steps of preparing the ideal soil for your purple roses.

First and foremost, it is crucial to choose a well-draining soil that is rich in organic matter. Purple roses thrive in soil that is slightly acidic, with a pH level between 6 and 6.5. You can test the soil's pH using a testing kit available at your local gardening store.

To improve drainage, add organic matter such as compost or well-rotted manure to the soil. This will not only provide essential nutrients but also enhance the soil's structure, allowing water to flow freely and preventing the roots from becoming waterlogged.

Before planting your purple roses, it is recommended to loosen the soil by tilling or digging. This will help the roots establish themselves easily and promote healthy growth. Remove any weeds or grass from the planting area to prevent competition for nutrients.

Once the soil is prepared, it is time to consider fertilization. Purple roses benefit from a slow-release balanced fertilizer, which provides a steady supply of nutrients throughout the growing season. Apply the fertilizer according to the manufacturer's instructions, taking care not to over-fertilize as this can damage the plants.

After planting your purple roses, mulching the soil is highly recommended. Mulch helps to retain moisture, suppress weeds, and regulate soil temperature. Organic mulch, such as wood chips or straw, is an excellent choice as it also adds nutrients to the soil as it breaks down over time.

In addition to soil preparation, it is crucial to provide adequate water and sunlight for your purple roses. They require at least six hours of direct sunlight each day and should be watered deeply and regularly, especially during dry periods.

By following these soil preparation tips, you can ensure that your purple roses receive the optimal growing conditions they need to thrive. With proper care and attention, your garden will be adorned with the mesmerizing beauty of these enchanting flowers.

Planting and Nurturing Purple Roses

Purple roses are a captivating addition to any garden, adding a touch of mystery and elegance. While they may not occur naturally in nature, they can be cultivated successfully with the right techniques and care. In this subchapter, we will explore the steps to growing and nurturing these stunning flowers, ensuring their vibrant hues shine through.

To begin, it is essential to select the right variety of purple roses for your garden. There are several options available, each with its unique shade of purple. Consider factors such as the size of the plant, the shape and fragrance of the blooms, and the overall hardiness of the variety. This will ensure that the roses you choose are suitable for your climate and gardening preferences.

When it comes to planting purple roses, it is crucial to prepare the soil adequately. Roses thrive in well-draining soil with a pH level between 6 and 7. Amend the soil with organic matter such as compost or well-rotted manure to improve fertility and drainage. Dig a hole slightly larger than the root ball of the rose, ensuring that the bud union is level with or slightly above the soil surface.

Once planted, purple roses require regular watering to establish strong root systems. Water deeply, ensuring the soil is moist but not waterlogged. Mulching around the base of the plants will help conserve moisture and suppress weeds. Additionally, applying a balanced rose fertilizer during the growing season will provide the necessary nutrients for healthy growth and abundant blooms.

Pruning is an essential aspect of nurturing purple roses. Regular pruning promotes new growth and helps maintain the shape and vigor of the plant. Remove any dead or damaged wood, as well as weak or crossing branches. Prune in early spring before new growth begins, and again in late summer to encourage a second flush of blooms.

To protect your purple roses from pests and diseases, it is important to monitor them regularly. Common pests such as aphids and spider mites can be controlled with insecticidal soaps or horticultural oils. Fungal diseases like black spot and powdery mildew can be prevented by ensuring good air circulation, proper spacing, and applying fungicides if necessary.

In conclusion, planting and nurturing purple roses requires careful attention to detail and proper care. By selecting the right variety, preparing the soil, watering, pruning, and protecting against pests and diseases, you can enjoy the beauty of these enchanting flowers in your garden. With their vibrant hues and unique charm, purple roses are sure to be a standout feature in any landscape.

Pruning and Maintaining Purple Roses

Purple roses are not only beautiful but also add a touch of elegance and mystique to any garden. To ensure that your purple roses thrive and continue to bloom abundantly, it is important to know how to properly prune and maintain them. In this subchapter, we will explore the essential techniques and tips for pruning and maintaining purple roses.

Pruning is an essential step in the care of any rose variety, and purple roses are no exception. The purpose of pruning is to remove dead, diseased, or damaged wood, encourage new growth, and shape the plant for optimal health and aesthetics. The best time to prune purple roses is in early spring, just before they start to grow again.

Start by removing any dead or weak canes, making clean cuts at a 45-degree angle about ¼ inch above an outward-facing bud. This will promote outward growth and prevent the center of the plant from becoming congested. Additionally, thin out any crossing or rubbing canes to improve air circulation and reduce the risk of disease.

After pruning, it is essential to provide proper care and maintenance to ensure the health and longevity of your purple roses. Regular watering is crucial, especially during dry spells or hot summer months. Aim to water deeply at the base of the plant to encourage deep root growth.

Mulching around the base of the roses with organic matter such as compost or wood chips will help retain moisture, suppress weeds, and regulate soil temperature. Remember to replenish the mulch annually to maintain its effectiveness.

Fertilizing purple roses is also essential for their overall health and vigor. Use a balanced rose fertilizer or organic alternatives, following the manufacturer's instructions. Apply the fertilizer around the base of the plant in early spring, just as new growth begins, and again in late spring or early summer.

Lastly, keep an eye out for common rose pests and diseases such as aphids, black spot, and powdery mildew. Inspect your purple roses regularly and take immediate action at the first sign of trouble. There are various organic and chemical options available for pest and disease control, so choose the method that suits your preferences and needs.

With proper pruning and maintenance, your purple roses will reward you with their stunning blooms and enchanting fragrance year after year. Follow these tips and techniques, and soon you will have a flourishing garden filled with vibrant and healthy purple roses.

Chapter 8: Nurturing Blue Roses Successfully

The Rare and Captivating Beauty of Blue Roses

Blue roses, with their enchanting hue and ethereal charm, have long captivated the hearts of gardeners and flower enthusiasts alike. While roses in various colors have been cultivated for centuries, the elusive blue rose remained a mystery until recent years. In this subchapter, we will explore the allure of blue roses, their unique characteristics, and the secrets to successfully cultivating these rare and captivating blooms.

Unlike other rose colors that occur naturally, blue roses are not found in nature. Their captivating beauty has been a subject of fascination and desire for centuries, leading to numerous attempts to create them through crossbreeding and genetic modification. After years of dedicated research and experimentation, horticulturalists were able to develop blue roses using a combination of traditional breeding techniques and biotechnology.

The mesmerizing blue color of these roses is achieved by introducing specific pigments into the petals through genetic modification. The result is a stunning range of blue shades, from deep indigo to delicate baby blue. The allure of blue roses lies not only in their rarity but also in the sense of mystery and tranquility they evoke.

To successfully nurture blue roses, certain considerations must be taken into account. These delicate blooms require well-drained soil with a slightly acidic pH level. Adequate sunlight is essential, but protection from harsh midday rays is recommended to prevent wilting. Regular watering is necessary to keep the soil moist but not waterlogged.

Blue roses also benefit from regular fertilization with a balanced rose fertilizer to promote healthy growth and vibrant blooms. Pruning is crucial to maintain the desired shape and prevent overcrowding, allowing for better air circulation and reducing the risk of diseases.

Creating a diverse range of colors in your rose garden is an exciting endeavor, and blue roses can be a striking addition. Imagine the beauty of a garden adorned with roses of all colors, from vibrant reds to delicate pinks, sunny yellows to regal purples, and finally, the elusive blue.

In conclusion, blue roses possess a rare and captivating beauty that adds a touch of magic to any garden. With proper care and attention, these extraordinary blooms can thrive and become the centerpiece of a diverse and enchanting rose collection. So, dare to dream and cultivate the mesmerizing allure of blue roses in your own garden.

Understanding the Challenges of Growing Blue Roses

Blue roses have always captivated gardeners and flower enthusiasts with their unique and elusive beauty. Often associated with mystery and enchantment, these elusive blooms are highly sought after by those looking to add a touch of rarity and elegance to their gardens. However, growing blue roses can be a challenging task that requires careful attention and specialized techniques.

One of the main challenges in growing blue roses is the fact that they do not exist naturally. Unlike other rose colors that can be found in nature, blue roses have been a product of extensive genetic modification and cross-breeding. This means that achieving the perfect shade of blue requires a deep understanding of genetics and a lot of patience.

The main obstacle in creating blue roses lies in the absence of the blue pigment delphinidin in roses. Delphinidin is responsible for the blue color in other flowers such as morning glories and hydrangeas, but it is not naturally present in roses. To overcome this challenge, breeders have developed various techniques, such as introducing genes from other blue-flowering plants into the rose's genetic makeup.

Another challenge in growing blue roses is maintaining the desired shade of blue. Blue pigments in roses tend to fade quickly, and exposure to sunlight can alter the color over time. To preserve the vibrant blue hue, it is important to provide the roses with the right amount of shade and protect them from direct sunlight. This can be achieved by planting them in partially shaded areas or using shade cloths or screens.

Furthermore, blue roses require specific soil conditions to thrive. They prefer slightly acidic soil with a pH level between 5.5 and 6.5. It is important to test the soil and make necessary amendments to ensure the ideal pH level for optimal growth. Additionally, blue roses benefit from regular fertilization with a balanced rose fertilizer to promote healthy growth and vibrant blooms.

In conclusion, growing blue roses can be a rewarding but challenging endeavor. It requires a deep understanding of genetics, specialized techniques, and careful attention to detail. By addressing the unique needs of blue roses, such as genetic modification, color preservation, and soil conditions, gardeners can successfully cultivate these elusive and enchanting blooms in their gardens. With patience and dedication, the allure of blue roses can be brought to life, adding a touch of magic to any floral display.

Soil Preparation for Blue Roses

Soil is the foundation of any successful garden, including one with blue roses. Proper soil preparation is essential for growing healthy and vibrant blue roses that will be the envy of every gardener. In this subchapter, we will explore the specific techniques and tips for preparing the soil to ensure optimal growth and blooming of blue roses.

Blue roses, although rare and exotic, require similar soil conditions as other rose varieties. However, there are a few additional considerations to keep in mind to enhance the blue coloration of the flowers. Let's dive into the soil preparation process.

First and foremost, blue roses thrive in slightly acidic soil with a pH level between 5.5 and 6.5. It is crucial to test the soil's pH and make necessary adjustments to achieve the desired acidity. You can add sulfur or iron sulfate to lower the pH or lime to raise it. Maintaining the correct pH level will provide the optimal conditions for blue pigment absorption in the roses.

Next, ensure the soil is well-drained to prevent waterlogging, which can lead to root rot and other diseases. Blue roses prefer moist but not overly wet soil. Incorporating organic matter, such as compost or well-rotted manure, will improve the soil's drainage and water-holding capacity.

Before planting blue roses, it is recommended to loosen the soil in the designated area. Remove any weeds, rocks, or debris from the site. Loosening the soil will promote healthy root development and allow the roots to penetrate easily.

To further enhance the soil's fertility, consider adding a slow-release granular rose fertilizer. Blue roses, like other rose varieties, are heavy feeders and require a nutrient-rich soil. Follow the manufacturer's instructions for the appropriate amount and timing of fertilizer application.

Lastly, mulching around the base of the blue roses will conserve moisture, suppress weed growth, and regulate soil temperature. Organic mulches, such as wood chips or straw, are excellent choices for rose beds. Apply a layer of mulch about 2-3 inches thick, ensuring it does not touch the stems to avoid rotting.

By following these soil preparation techniques, you will provide the ideal growing environment for blue roses. Remember, maintaining the correct soil pH, ensuring proper drainage, enriching the soil with organic matter, and applying fertilizer and mulch will set the stage for beautiful and vibrant blue roses in your garden. Happy gardening!

Planting and Caring for Blue Roses

Blue roses have long captivated the imagination of gardeners and flower enthusiasts alike. With their elusive and enchanting beauty, they add a touch of mystery and uniqueness to any garden. In this subchapter, we will explore the secrets to successfully planting and caring for these elusive blooms.

To start, it is important to note that blue roses do not occur naturally in nature. However, through careful breeding and genetic modification, horticulturists have been able to create varieties that mimic the appearance of blue. These blue roses are often referred to as "blue-mauve" or "lavender" in color.

When it comes to planting blue roses, choose a sunny spot in your garden with well-draining soil. Blue roses thrive in full sun, so make sure they receive at least six hours of direct sunlight each day. Prepare the soil by adding organic matter, such as compost or well-rotted manure, to improve drainage and fertility.

Before planting, soak the rose bush in water for a few hours to rehydrate the roots. Dig a hole that is wide and deep enough to accommodate the roots comfortably. Place the rose bush in the hole, making sure the bud union (the swollen area where the rose was grafted onto the rootstock) is level with or slightly above the soil surface. Backfill the hole with soil, firming it gently around the roots.

Once planted, water the rose thoroughly and apply a layer of organic mulch around the base to conserve moisture and suppress weeds. Blue roses require regular watering, especially during dry spells. It is important to keep the soil consistently moist but not waterlogged. Avoid wetting the foliage, as this can lead to disease and fungal problems.

Fertilize your blue roses regularly during the growing season with a balanced rose fertilizer. Follow the instructions on the package for the correct application rate. Pruning is also essential for maintaining the health and shape of your blue roses. In late winter or early spring, remove any dead or damaged wood and shape the plant as desired.

Remember that blue roses are more delicate than other varieties, and they require extra care. Monitor them closely for any signs of pests or diseases, such as aphids or black spot. Treat any issues promptly to prevent them from spreading.

In conclusion, growing blue roses can be a rewarding and magical experience. With the right care and attention, you can enjoy the beauty of these elusive blooms in your own garden. So go ahead and embrace the challenge of cultivating blue roses, and let their enchanting presence transform your garden into a haven of unique colors and fragrances.

Pruning and Training Techniques for Blue Roses

Blue roses are known for their unique and captivating beauty. While they may not occur naturally in nature, with the right techniques, you can successfully cultivate and nurture blue roses in your own garden. In this subchapter, we will explore the various pruning and training techniques that will help you achieve the best results with your blue roses.

Pruning is an essential task when it comes to maintaining the health and shape of your blue rose bushes. It is recommended to prune your roses during the dormant season, which is usually in late winter or early spring. Begin by removing any dead or damaged wood, making clean cuts just above a healthy bud. This will encourage new growth and improve the overall appearance of the plant.

When it comes to training blue roses, it is important to provide them with proper support. Blue roses tend to have softer stems compared to other rose varieties, making them more prone to bending or breaking. Use stakes or trellises to support the branches and prevent them from drooping or snapping under the weight of the blossoms.

Another technique that can enhance the growth and color intensity of your blue roses is disbudding. This involves removing some of the buds from the plant, allowing the remaining buds to receive more nutrients and energy. By removing the smaller or weaker buds, the plant can direct its resources towards producing larger and more vibrant flowers.

In addition to pruning and training, it is crucial to provide your blue roses with the right care and conditions. Blue roses thrive in well-draining soil with a slightly acidic pH level. Regular watering is important, but be mindful not to overwater, as this can lead to root rot. Applying a layer of mulch around the base of the plant can help retain moisture and regulate temperature.

Lastly, don't forget to fertilize your blue roses regularly to promote healthy growth and vibrant blooms. Choose a balanced rose fertilizer or one specifically formulated for blue flowers. Follow the instructions on the package for the correct application rate and frequency.

By following these pruning and training techniques, you can successfully cultivate and nurture stunning blue roses in your garden. Remember to provide them with the right care, and soon you will be rewarded with a spectacular display of these extraordinary flowers.

Chapter 9: Growing Multi-Colored Roses

The Vibrancy and Playfulness of Multi-Colored Roses

When it comes to roses, many gardeners often think of the classic red or white varieties. However, there is a whole world of vibrant and playful multi-colored roses waiting to be explored. These unique and eye-catching blooms can bring a burst of color to any garden, adding a touch of whimsy and charm.

Growing multi-colored roses may seem like a daunting task, but with the right techniques and care, you can successfully cultivate these beautiful blooms. The key to achieving vibrant hues and a diverse range of colors lies in selecting the right rose varieties and providing them with the optimal growing conditions.

One of the most important factors to consider when growing multi-colored roses is choosing the right soil and fertilizers. Roses thrive in well-draining soil rich in organic matter. By amending your soil with compost or well-rotted manure, you can create the perfect environment for your roses to flourish.

In addition to soil preparation, proper watering and sunlight are crucial for the health and vibrancy of multi-colored roses. These roses generally require at least six hours of direct sunlight each day to produce their stunning colors. However, it's important to avoid excessive heat, as this can cause the petals to fade or wilt.

When it comes to selecting multi-colored rose varieties, there are numerous options to choose from. Some popular choices include the 'Rainbow Sorbet' rose, which showcases a delightful blend of pinks, yellows, and oranges, and the 'Scentimental' rose, which features striking red and white striped petals. By incorporating these unique varieties into your garden, you can create a truly mesmerizing display of colors.

Once you have successfully grown your multi-colored roses, it's important to provide them with the necessary care and maintenance. Regular pruning, deadheading, and fertilizing will help ensure healthy growth and abundant blooms. Additionally, certain varieties, such as black roses, require special care to maintain their dark and mysterious hues. These roses benefit from extra sunlight and specific fertilizers formulated for dark-colored flowers.

In conclusion, growing multi-colored roses can bring a sense of vibrancy and playfulness to your garden. With the right techniques and care, you can cultivate a diverse range of colors, from soft pinks to bold purples and even rare black varieties. By incorporating these unique blooms into your garden, you can create a stunning display that will surely captivate any observer. So, why not add a touch of whimsy and charm to your garden with the vibrant and playful beauty of multi-colored roses?

Selecting the Best Multi-Colored Rose Varieties

One of the most captivating aspects of growing roses is the opportunity to cultivate multi-colored varieties that showcase a stunning array of hues. As a gardener, you can create a vibrant and diverse rose garden by carefully selecting the best multi-colored rose varieties. In this subchapter, we will explore the different types of multi-colored roses and provide tips on how to grow them successfully.

Multi-colored roses, also known as bi-color or striped roses, are a delightful addition to any garden. These roses feature petals with two or more distinct colors that create a striking visual impact. When selecting multi-colored rose varieties, consider the overall color scheme of your garden and choose roses that complement or contrast with the existing blooms.

One popular multi-colored rose variety is the 'Joseph's Coat' rose. Its petals display a mesmerizing combination of red, orange, and yellow, creating a stunning gradient effect. Another exquisite choice is the 'Scentimental' rose, which showcases deep red and white stripes, adding a touch of elegance to any garden.

To grow multi-colored roses successfully, it is essential to provide them with the right conditions. Choose a sunny location for your rose garden, as roses thrive in full sunlight. Ensure that the soil is well-draining and rich in organic matter. Before planting, amend the soil with compost or well-rotted manure to improve its fertility.

Proper watering is crucial for the health and vitality of multi-colored roses. Water deeply and thoroughly, making sure the soil is evenly moist but not waterlogged. Avoid overhead watering, as this can lead to disease and fungal issues. Instead, water at the base of the plant to keep the foliage dry.

Pruning is another essential aspect of rose care, especially for multi-colored varieties. Regular pruning helps maintain the shape and vigor of the plant while promoting new growth and abundant blooms. Aim to prune your roses in early spring, before new growth emerges.

In conclusion, growing multi-colored roses can add a captivating touch to your garden. By selecting the best varieties and providing them with proper care, you can create a stunning display of vibrant and diverse blooms. With attention to detail and a little TLC, your multi-colored rose garden will become a true masterpiece.

Soil Preparation for Multi-Colored Roses

Growing multi-colored roses can be an exciting and rewarding experience for gardeners who are passionate about creating a diverse and vibrant rose garden. However, to achieve the best results, it is crucial to prepare the soil properly. In this subchapter, we will guide you through the essential steps of soil preparation for multi-colored roses, ensuring that your plants thrive and produce beautiful blooms in a variety of colors.

First and foremost, it is important to choose the right location for your rose garden. Roses require at least six hours of direct sunlight each day, so select a spot that receives ample sunlight. Once you have identified the perfect location, it's time to prepare the soil.

Start by removing any weeds or grass from the area. Dig up the soil to a depth of about 12 inches, breaking up any clumps and removing rocks or debris. This will allow the roots of your roses to penetrate the soil easily and establish strong, healthy plants.

Next, enrich the soil with organic matter such as compost or well-rotted manure. This will improve the soil structure, drainage, and nutrient content. Spread a layer of organic matter over the soil and work it in with a garden fork or tiller. Aim for a depth of about 4-6 inches.

Now it's time to test the soil pH. Roses prefer a slightly acidic soil with a pH range of 6.0 to 6.5. You can easily test the pH using a soil testing kit available at garden centers. If the pH is too high, you can lower it by adding elemental sulfur or peat moss. Lime can be added to raise the pH if it is too low.

Once the soil is prepared and the pH is adjusted, it's time to add some nutrients. Roses are heavy feeders, so incorporate a balanced rose fertilizer into the soil. Follow the manufacturer's instructions for application rates. Additionally, consider adding bone meal or rock phosphate to provide phosphorus, which promotes root development and flowering.

Finally, water the soil thoroughly to ensure it is evenly moist. This will help settle the soil and remove any air pockets. Allow the soil to settle for a few days before planting your multi-colored roses.

By following these soil preparation guidelines, you will create an optimal growing environment for your multi-colored roses. Remember to continue providing regular care and maintenance to keep your roses healthy and vibrant. Happy gardening!

Planting and Nurturing Multi-Colored Roses

Roses are undoubtedly one of the most beautiful and cherished flowers in any garden. From vibrant reds to delicate pinks and sunny yellows, roses come in a myriad of colors, each with its unique charm. As a gardener, you have the opportunity to create a stunning display of multi-colored roses that will captivate the senses and bring joy to your garden. In this subchapter, we will explore the art of planting and nurturing multi-colored roses, providing you with the knowledge and tips you need to create a diverse rose garden.

To begin, it is essential to select a variety of roses with different colors. Look for varieties that are known for their vibrant hues, such as the deep red 'Mr. Lincoln,' the delicate white 'Iceberg,' or the striking yellow 'Golden Celebration.' Additionally, consider adding rare and exotic rose varieties to add a touch of uniqueness to your garden.

When it comes to planting multi-colored roses, the key is to provide them with the right conditions. Roses thrive in well-drained soil enriched with organic matter. Choose a sunny spot in your garden that receives at least six hours of direct sunlight daily. Dig a hole that is wide and deep enough to accommodate the rose's root ball, ensuring that the bud union is level with or slightly above the soil surface.

After planting, it is crucial to provide your roses with proper care and attention. Regular watering is essential, especially during dry spells. Mulching around the base of the plants will help conserve moisture and suppress weed growth. Fertilize your roses regularly with a balanced rose food to promote healthy growth and abundant blooms.

To maintain the vibrant colors of your multi-colored roses, deadhead faded flowers regularly. This will encourage the plant to produce more blooms and prevent the development of rose hips. Pruning is also essential for maintaining the shape and health of your roses. Remove any dead or diseased wood and prune back any overgrown branches in early spring.

It is worth noting that some rose varieties, such as black roses and other dark-colored varieties, require special care. These roses are more prone to disease and require extra attention to ensure their health and longevity. Regular inspections for pests and diseases, as well as proper pruning and fertilization, are crucial for these varieties.

By following these tips and techniques, you can create a magnificent rose garden bursting with a diverse range of colors. Whether you choose to grow red, white, pink, yellow, purple, or even blue roses, your garden will be a feast for the eyes and a source of endless joy for any gardener. Embrace the beauty of multi-colored roses and watch your garden come alive with their enchanting hues.

Pruning and Maintaining Multi-Colored Roses

As a gardener, one of the most rewarding experiences is growing and maintaining vibrant, multi-colored roses in your garden. These beautiful flowers add a touch of elegance and diversity to any landscape. In this subchapter, we will explore the best practices for pruning and maintaining multi-colored roses, ensuring their health and beauty year after year.

Pruning is an essential step in maintaining the overall health and appearance of your multi-colored roses. It helps promote new growth, enhances flowering, and keeps the plant in shape. The ideal time to prune your roses is during late winter or early spring, just before new growth begins. Start by removing any dead or damaged branches, making clean cuts at a 45-degree angle. This will prevent the spread of diseases and encourage healthy regrowth.

When it comes to multi-colored roses, it is important to maintain their distinct colors. To do this, you must remove any branches or shoots that are producing flowers of a different color. This will help preserve the integrity of each rose's unique hues and prevent them from blending together.

Regular maintenance is key to ensuring the long-term health and vitality of your multi-colored roses. This includes fertilizing, watering, and protecting them from pests and diseases. Use a balanced rose fertilizer to provide the necessary nutrients and promote vigorous growth. Water your roses deeply but infrequently, allowing the soil to dry out slightly between waterings. This will prevent root rot and encourage the development of a strong root system.

Pests and diseases can pose a threat to your multi-colored roses, so it is important to be vigilant. Regularly inspect your plants for signs of aphids, spider mites, or black spot. If you notice any issues, treat them promptly with organic or chemical pesticides to prevent further damage.

In conclusion, pruning and maintaining multi-colored roses requires careful attention and dedication. By following these tips, you can ensure that your roses remain healthy, vibrant, and true to their unique colors. Incorporating these practices into your gardening routine will allow you to create a stunning display of multi-colored roses that will be the envy of every garden enthusiast.

Chapter 10: Tips for Cultivating Rare and Exotic Rose Varieties

The Allure and Rarity of Exotic Rose Varieties

Roses have long been regarded as the epitome of beauty and elegance, but there is something truly captivating about the allure and rarity of exotic rose varieties. These unique and extraordinary blooms possess an enchanting charm that sets them apart from their more common counterparts. In this subchapter, we will explore the fascinating world of exotic roses and delve into the secrets of growing these precious gems.

One of the most sought-after exotic rose varieties is the elusive black rose. Its mysterious and velvety petals have captivated the imaginations of gardeners for centuries. While truly black roses do not exist in nature, there are dark-colored varieties that can create a similar effect. We will reveal the tips and techniques for cultivating black roses, including the importance of selecting the right cultivar and providing them with optimal growing conditions.

Red roses, the timeless symbol of love and passion, hold a special place in the hearts of many gardeners. We will share expert advice on how to grow vibrant and healthy red roses, covering everything from soil preparation to pruning techniques. Whether you desire a classic red rose or a deep crimson beauty, our tips will help you achieve stunning results.

For those who prefer the purity and elegance of white roses, we have invaluable tips for creating a breathtaking display of these delicate blooms. We will guide you through the process of selecting the right white rose varieties for your garden and provide insights into their unique care requirements.

Pink roses, with their soft and romantic hues, are a favorite among gardeners. We will explore the diverse range of pink rose shades and offer advice on how to cultivate these charming beauties. From pale blush to vibrant fuchsia, we will reveal the secrets to growing pink roses that will add a touch of romance to any garden.

But our exploration of exotic roses does not stop there. We will also delve into the world of yellow roses, with their vibrant and sunny disposition, and share techniques for cultivating purple roses that exude an air of mystery and royalty. For the truly adventurous, we will even uncover the secrets to nurturing blue roses, a rarity that has long eluded rose enthusiasts.

In addition to exploring the cultivation of specific exotic rose varieties, we will offer tips for growing multi-colored roses, creating a rose garden with a diverse range of colors that will dazzle the senses. We will also provide special care instructions for black roses and other dark-colored varieties to ensure their health and longevity.

Join us on this journey through the captivating world of exotic roses, and discover the secrets to growing these rare and enchanting blooms. Whether you are a seasoned gardener or just starting out, this subchapter is a must-read for anyone seeking to create a garden filled with the allure and rarity of exotic rose varieties.

Researching and Sourcing Rare and Exotic Roses

When it comes to growing roses, gardeners are always on the lookout for unique and extraordinary varieties. While red, white, and pink roses are commonly found in many gardens, there is a growing interest in cultivating rare and exotic roses that display a diverse range of colors. In this subchapter, we will explore how to research and source these elusive beauties to create a truly remarkable rose garden.

One of the first steps in finding rare and exotic roses is thorough research. Begin by exploring online catalogs, gardening forums, and websites dedicated to rose enthusiasts. These sources often provide valuable information about different rose varieties, including their colors, growth habits, and availability. Take note of any rare or exotic roses that catch your eye and make a list of potential suppliers or nurseries.

Once you have identified the rose varieties you desire, it's time to source them. Start by contacting local nurseries and garden centers to see if they carry the specific roses you are looking for. If not, they may be able to order them for you or provide recommendations on where to find them. Additionally, reach out to specialty rose nurseries that specialize in rare and exotic varieties. These nurseries often have a wide selection and can offer expert advice on cultivation and care.

Another option for sourcing rare and exotic roses is through rose societies and clubs. These organizations are passionate about roses and often have members who are avid collectors. By joining such groups, you can tap into a network of knowledgeable gardeners who may be willing to share or trade rare rose cuttings or plants.

When purchasing rare roses, be prepared to invest both time and money. These varieties are often more expensive and can have limited availability. It's essential to buy from reputable sources to ensure you are getting genuine plants. Look for nurseries that provide detailed descriptions and photos of the roses they offer, and consider reading reviews or seeking recommendations from experienced gardeners.

In conclusion, researching and sourcing rare and exotic roses requires dedication and a keen eye for detail. By conducting thorough research, reaching out to nurseries and rose societies, and investing in quality plants, gardeners can create a rose garden that showcases a diverse range of colors and rare varieties. Remember to be patient and persistent in your search, and soon you will be rewarded with the beauty and elegance of these extraordinary roses.

Special Soil and Growing Conditions for Exotic Roses

Growing exotic roses can be a rewarding and exciting experience for any gardener. These unique and rare varieties add a touch of elegance and intrigue to any garden. However, to successfully cultivate these magnificent blooms, it is crucial to understand their special soil and growing conditions. In this subchapter, we will explore the specific requirements for growing exotic roses of all colors, including black roses.

Exotic roses thrive in well-draining soil that is rich in organic matter. It is essential to prepare the soil before planting by incorporating compost and aged manure to improve its fertility and structure. Adding perlite or vermiculite can also enhance drainage, preventing waterlogged roots and diseases.

When it comes to pH levels, most exotic roses prefer slightly acidic to neutral soil, with a pH range of 6.0 to 7.0. However, it is crucial to research the specific requirements of each variety, as some may have different preferences. Conduct a soil test to determine the pH levels and adjust accordingly.

In terms of sunlight, exotic roses generally require full sun to thrive and produce abundant blooms. Provide at least six hours of direct sunlight daily, ensuring the plants receive adequate light for photosynthesis and healthy growth. If your garden has limited sun exposure, consider planting them in containers that can be moved to sunnier spots throughout the day.

Watering is a crucial aspect of nurturing exotic roses. While they require regular watering, it is vital to avoid overwatering, as excess moisture can lead to root rot and other fungal diseases. Water deeply at the base of the plants, ensuring the soil is evenly moist but not saturated. Using mulch around the base of the plants can help retain moisture and suppress weed growth.

In addition to the general care guidelines, each color of exotic rose may have specific requirements. For example, black roses and other dark-colored varieties benefit from extra attention to prevent sunburn on their petals. Applying a light layer of shade cloth or placing them in partially shaded areas during the hottest parts of the day can help protect their delicate blooms.

By understanding the special soil and growing conditions for exotic roses, gardeners can successfully cultivate these rare and beautiful varieties. Whether you are growing red, white, pink, yellow, purple, blue, or multi-colored roses, providing the right soil, sunlight, water, and care will result in vibrant and healthy plants. With dedication and a little bit of knowledge, you can create a stunning rose garden that showcases the diversity of colors and cultivates rare and exotic rose varieties.

Planting and Caring for Rare and Exotic Roses

Roses are undoubtedly one of the most beloved and sought-after flowers in the world. Their beauty, fragrance, and symbolism make them a popular choice for gardeners of all levels. While traditional rose varieties like red, white, and pink are widely available, there is a whole world of rare and exotic roses waiting to be explored. In this subchapter, we will delve into the art of growing and caring for these unique varieties, from black roses to multi-colored blooms.

When it comes to planting rare and exotic roses, it is essential to choose the right location. These roses often require specific conditions to thrive, so ensure that the chosen spot receives adequate sunlight, has well-draining soil, and offers protection from strong winds.

Additionally, consider incorporating organic matter into the soil to improve its fertility and drainage.

Before planting, it is crucial to prepare the roses for their new home. Soak the roots of bare-root roses in water for a few hours to rehydrate them. For potted roses, gently loosen the root ball before planting. Dig a hole wide and deep enough to accommodate the roots, making sure that the bud union (the swollen area where the rose was grafted) is level with or slightly above the soil surface.

Once planted, caring for rare and exotic roses involves regular maintenance. Water deeply and consistently, providing enough moisture to keep the soil evenly moist but not waterlogged. Mulching around the base of the rose can help retain moisture and suppress weeds. Fertilize regularly with a balanced rose fertilizer to promote healthy growth and abundant blooms.

Different rose varieties may require specific care instructions. For instance, black roses and other dark-colored varieties benefit from extra attention. They tend to be more susceptible to heat stress, so consider providing them with some shade during the hottest parts of the day. Additionally, these roses are prone to mildew, so be vigilant in monitoring for any signs of disease and treat promptly if necessary.

In conclusion, growing rare and exotic roses can be a rewarding and exciting endeavor for gardeners. By carefully selecting the right location, preparing the plants for planting, and providing consistent care, you can enjoy the beauty of these unique blooms in your garden. Remember to tailor your care routine to the specific needs of each variety, and soon you will have a rose garden filled with an array of vibrant colors and exquisite scents.

Overcoming Challenges in Growing Rare and Exotic Roses

Growing rare and exotic roses can be a rewarding experience for any gardener. However, it is not without its challenges. In this subchapter, we will discuss some common obstacles faced by gardeners when trying to cultivate these unique varieties and provide tips on how to overcome them.

One of the biggest challenges in growing rare and exotic roses is finding the right variety. Unlike more common rose cultivars, these unique roses are not readily available at local nurseries or garden centers. Gardeners may have to search online or visit specialty rose nurseries to find the specific varieties they desire. It requires patience and persistence, but the effort is well worth it for the beauty and uniqueness these roses bring to the garden.

Another challenge is ensuring proper care for these rare and exotic roses. Many of these varieties have specific requirements when it comes to sunlight, soil pH, and watering. It is important to research and understand the specific needs of each variety before planting. Some roses may require more attention and care than others, but with the right knowledge and dedication, any gardener can successfully cultivate these unique blooms.

Disease and pest management is also a crucial aspect of growing rare and exotic roses. These varieties may be more susceptible to certain diseases and pests compared to more common rose cultivars. It is important to regularly inspect the plants for any signs of disease or pest infestation and take appropriate action. Regular pruning, proper watering, and good hygiene practices can help prevent and control these issues.

Furthermore, climate can pose a challenge for growing rare and exotic roses. Some varieties may not be well-suited to certain climates or may require extra protection during harsh winters or scorching summers. It is important to choose varieties that are more adaptable to the local climate or provide necessary shelter and insulation to protect the plants from extreme weather conditions.

In conclusion, growing rare and exotic roses may present its fair share of challenges, but with proper research, care, and attention, any gardener can overcome them. The key is to be patient, persistent, and willing to adapt to the specific needs of these unique varieties. With time and effort, the rewards of cultivating these rare and exotic roses will be well worth it, as they add a touch of beauty and intrigue to any garden.

Chapter 11: Creating a Rose Garden with a Diverse Range of Colors

Designing and Planning Your Rose Garden

Creating a beautiful and vibrant rose garden requires careful planning and thoughtful design. Whether you are a seasoned gardener or just starting out, this subchapter will provide you with valuable tips and techniques to help you grow roses of all colors, including rare and exotic varieties. From red to black, yellow to purple, pink to blue, we will cover everything you need to know to cultivate a diverse range of roses in your garden.

Before you begin, it is important to assess your garden's conditions and choose the right location for your roses. Roses thrive in full sun, so select an area that receives at least six hours of direct sunlight each day. Additionally, ensure that the soil is well-draining and rich in organic matter. If your soil is heavy clay or sandy, consider amending it with compost or well-rotted manure to improve its texture and fertility.

Once you have chosen the perfect spot, it's time to design your rose garden. Start by sketching out a plan, taking into consideration the size, shape, and color of the roses you want to grow. Consider planting taller varieties in the back to create depth and visual interest. Group roses of similar colors together to create stunning color blocks, or mix different shades for a more varied and eclectic display.

When it comes to caring for your roses, each color may require slightly different techniques. Red roses, for example, benefit from regular pruning to encourage more blooms, while white roses may be more susceptible to diseases and require careful monitoring. Yellow roses, on the other hand, can benefit from regular feeding to enhance their vibrant hues.

For those interested in growing rare and exotic rose varieties, it is important to research their specific needs and requirements. Some may require specialized care, such as protection from extreme temperatures or specific soil conditions. However, the effort will be well worth it when you see these unique and stunning roses blooming in your garden.

Lastly, special attention should be given to black roses and other dark-colored varieties. These roses are known for their unique beauty, but they also need extra care. Regular watering, proper fertilization, and protection from harsh sunlight are essential to keep their dark petals healthy and vibrant.

Designing and planning your rose garden is an exciting and rewarding process. With careful consideration of your garden's conditions and the specific needs of each rose variety, you can create a stunning display of roses in all colors imaginable. By following the tips and techniques provided in this subchapter, you will be well on your way to cultivating a rose garden that is the envy of all gardeners.

Combining Different Rose Colors and Varieties

Roses are not only known for their exquisite beauty and fragrance but also for the wide range of colors they come in. From vibrant reds to delicate pinks, sunny yellows to regal purples, and even the elusive black roses, there is a rose color for every gardener's taste. In this subchapter, we will explore the art of combining different rose colors and varieties to create a stunning and diverse rose garden.

When it comes to combining rose colors, the possibilities are endless. One popular technique is to create a color scheme, using complementary or contrasting colors to create a visually striking effect. For example, pairing red roses with white roses can create a classic and elegant look, while combining pink and purple roses can bring about a romantic and dreamy ambiance.

To create a garden with a diverse range of colors, consider planting roses from different color families. For instance, you can mix red, pink, yellow, and purple roses together to create a vibrant and eye-catching display. Additionally, incorporating multi-colored roses, which have petals with more than one color, can add an element of surprise and intrigue to your garden.

When cultivating rare and exotic rose varieties, it is essential to pay extra attention to their specific needs. These roses often require special care and maintenance to thrive. Ensure you understand their unique requirements, such as soil pH, sunlight exposure, and watering needs, to provide the best conditions for their growth.

Black roses and other dark-colored varieties are particularly intriguing and mysterious. To ensure their success, it is crucial to give them the special care they need. These roses tend to prefer full sun exposure and well-drained soil. Regular pruning and fertilizing can also help promote healthy growth and vibrant blooms.

By combining different rose colors and varieties, you can create a captivating and enchanting rose garden that will be the envy of all gardeners. Experiment with different combinations, play with color schemes, and don't be afraid to try new and unique rose varieties. With a little knowledge and a lot of passion, you can create a rose garden that is a true work of art.

Companion Plants and Landscaping Ideas for Rose Gardens

Creating a beautiful and vibrant rose garden goes beyond just growing roses of different colors. By incorporating companion plants and thoughtful landscaping ideas, you can enhance the overall beauty and health of your rose garden. In this subchapter, we will explore various companion plants and landscaping ideas that can complement your roses and create a stunning display of colors and textures.

Companion plants play a crucial role in rose gardens. They not only provide visual interest but can also attract beneficial insects, deter pests, and improve soil health. Some popular companion plants for roses include lavender, catmint, geraniums, and salvia. Lavender, with its soothing fragrance and purple blooms, pairs well with roses of all colors. Catmint and geraniums, known for their long blooming period, add a pop of color to the garden while attracting pollinators. Salvia, with its vibrant blue flowers, creates a striking contrast when planted alongside roses of any hue.

In terms of landscaping ideas, consider creating a focal point by grouping roses of similar colors together. For instance, you can create a bed of red roses that demands attention or a section dedicated to yellow roses for a cheerful and vibrant display. Alternatively, you can opt for a mixed bed, where roses of different colors are interplanted, creating a beautiful tapestry of colors.

To add height and dimension to your rose garden, incorporate climbing roses and trellises. Climbing roses can be trained to grow up trellises, fences, or arches, adding vertical interest and creating a sense of depth in the garden. Additionally, consider adding low-growing groundcovers such as creeping thyme or creeping phlox around the base of your rose bushes. These plants not only suppress weeds but also provide a lush carpet of color that complements the roses above.

When designing your rose garden, don't forget to consider the specific needs of black roses and other dark-colored varieties. These roses require extra care due to their unique pigmentation. Ensure they receive ample sunlight and proper pruning to maintain their dark color and prevent fading.

By incorporating companion plants and implementing thoughtful landscaping ideas, you can create a rose garden that is not only visually stunning but also supports the health and vitality of your roses. Experiment with different combinations and explore the endless possibilities of creating a diverse range of colors and textures in your rose garden. With a little planning and creativity, your rose garden will become a true masterpiece.

Creating a Harmonious Color Palette in Your Rose Garden

One of the most enchanting aspects of growing roses is the vast array of colors they come in. From vibrant reds to delicate pinks, and even rare black roses, there is a color to suit every gardener's taste. However, when it comes to creating a harmonious color palette in your rose garden, it's important to take some factors into consideration. In this subchapter, we will explore tips and techniques for cultivating a rose garden with a diverse range of colors that blend seamlessly together.

When planning your rose garden, it's essential to consider the overall theme or mood you want to create. Do you prefer a romantic and soft color palette, or are you more drawn to bold and vibrant hues? Once you determine your desired aesthetic, you can start selecting roses that match your vision.

To create a harmonious color palette, it's helpful to choose roses that fall within the same color family. For example, if you want a garden with warm and fiery tones, opt for reds, oranges, and yellows. On the other hand, if you prefer a serene and calming atmosphere, choose roses in shades of pink, lavender, and white.

Another technique for achieving a harmonious color palette is to play with different shades of the same color. For instance, you can combine light pink roses with deeper shades of magenta or mauve. This creates depth and visual interest while maintaining a cohesive color scheme.

Don't be afraid to experiment with multi-colored roses as well. These varieties can add a unique and eye-catching element to your garden. Look for roses with petals that blend multiple colors together, such as roses with pink and white stripes or those with yellow and orange gradients.

When cultivating a rose garden with rare and exotic varieties, it's important to provide them with special care. Black roses and other dark-colored varieties, in particular, require specific attention. They often prefer well-draining soil and benefit from regular fertilization. Additionally, they may need extra protection from harsh sunlight to prevent their unique colors from fading.

In conclusion, creating a harmonious color palette in your rose garden is a delightful endeavor that allows you to showcase the beauty of different hues. By choosing roses that complement each other and experimenting with various shades and multi-colored varieties, you can create a visually stunning and cohesive garden. Remember to provide special care for rare and exotic roses, especially dark-colored varieties, to ensure their colors remain vibrant. With these tips and techniques, you will be well on your way to cultivating a breathtaking rose garden that will be the envy of all gardeners.

Maintaining and Enhancing the Beauty of Your Rose Garden

Your rose garden is a canvas of vibrant colors and delicate fragrances, a place where beauty flourishes. As a gardener, it is crucial to understand the techniques and tips for maintaining and enhancing the splendor of your roses. In this subchapter, we will explore various aspects of rose care, from growing specific colors to cultivating rare and exotic varieties.

To begin with, let's delve into the secrets of growing roses of all colors, including the much sought-after black roses. Each color requires specific attention, and understanding their unique needs is crucial for their well-being. Whether it's red roses symbolizing love and passion, white roses representing purity and innocence, or pink roses in their various shades radiating elegance and grace, we will provide you with valuable tips to help them thrive.

If you desire a garden adorned with yellow roses in vibrant hues, we will guide you through the cultivation process. Similarly, we will unveil the techniques for nurturing purple roses, a symbol of enchantment and royalty. Furthermore, we will explore the elusive world of blue roses, teaching you how to successfully grow these unique beauties.

For those who crave multi-colored roses, we have some exciting insights to offer. Creating a rose garden with a diverse range of colors requires careful planning and consideration. We will provide you with the knowledge to create harmonious blends and captivating combinations.

If you're a gardener with a penchant for rare and exotic rose varieties, our tips for cultivating these gems will prove invaluable. From understanding their specific requirements to ensuring their optimum growth, we will equip you with the necessary knowledge to care for these precious blooms.

Lastly, we will address special care for black roses and other dark-colored varieties. These mysterious and enchanting flowers require extra attention to maintain their intense pigmentation. We will share with you some expert techniques to keep them healthy and vibrant.

Maintaining and enhancing the beauty of your rose garden is an ongoing process. With our comprehensive guide, you will gain the expertise needed to nurture your roses into stunning masterpieces. So grab your gardening tools and get ready to embark on a journey of cultivating beautiful roses in an array of colors, including those rare and exotic varieties that will make your garden the envy of all.

Remember, the key to a truly magnificent rose garden lies in your dedication, patience, and love for these enchanting flowers. Happy gardening!

Chapter 12: Special Care for Black Roses and Other Dark-Colored Varieties

Understanding the Unique Needs of Dark-Colored Roses

Growing roses of all colors can be a rewarding and fulfilling experience for gardeners. Each color represents a unique beauty and charm that adds flair to any garden. However, when it comes to dark-colored roses, such as black and deep purple varieties, there are some specific needs that must be understood and met in order to ensure their successful growth and blooming. In this subchapter, we will explore these unique needs and provide valuable tips for cultivating these exquisite dark-colored roses.

Dark-colored roses, particularly black roses, require special care due to their intense pigmentation. One of the key factors to consider is sunlight exposure. Unlike other roses, dark-colored varieties thrive best when they receive at least six hours of direct sunlight each day. This exposure to sunlight helps in enhancing their rich color and promoting healthy growth. Therefore, it is essential to choose a location in your garden that receives ample sunlight for planting these roses.

Another crucial aspect to focus on is soil composition. Dark-colored roses thrive in well-draining soil that is rich in organic matter. Adding compost or well-rotted manure to the soil can help improve its texture and fertility. Additionally, regular watering is important to keep the soil moist but not waterlogged. A deep watering once a week is usually sufficient, but you should adjust the frequency based on the weather conditions and the moisture needs of your specific roses.

Pruning is also vital for maintaining the health and appearance of dark-colored roses. Regular pruning not only helps in shaping the plants but also promotes new growth and enhances blooming. It is recommended to prune these roses in early spring, removing dead or diseased wood and thinning out any overcrowded branches.

Lastly, dark-colored roses, especially black roses, require extra attention to prevent them from fading or losing their color. Applying a layer of mulch around the base of the plants can help in retaining moisture and protecting the roses from extreme temperatures. Additionally, providing adequate airflow and avoiding overhead watering can minimize the risk of fungal diseases that may affect the overall health and color of the roses.

Understanding the unique needs of dark-colored roses is essential for gardeners seeking to add these captivating varieties to their collection. By following the tips and techniques discussed in this subchapter, you will be well-equipped to grow and nurture these rare and exquisite roses, creating a garden that showcases the beauty and diversity of colors nature has to offer.

Sunlight and Temperature Considerations for Dark-Colored Roses

When it comes to growing dark-colored roses, such as the elusive black roses or deep purple varieties, there are specific considerations to keep in mind regarding sunlight and temperature. Understanding these factors will help you create the optimal conditions for your dark-colored roses to thrive and showcase their stunning hues.

Sunlight plays a crucial role in the color intensity of roses. Dark-colored roses require a significant amount of direct sunlight to develop their rich pigmentation. Ideally, they should receive at least six hours of direct sunlight per day. However, in hotter climates, it is essential to strike a balance between providing enough sunlight and protecting the roses from scorching heat. In such cases, consider providing partial shade during the hottest part of the day to prevent sunburn and wilting.

Temperature also plays a significant role in the growth and color development of dark-colored roses. These roses tend to thrive in moderate temperatures, ideally between 60 to 75 degrees Fahrenheit. Extreme heat can cause the petals to fade or wilt prematurely, while chilly temperatures can hinder their growth. It is essential to monitor the weather conditions and take appropriate measures to protect your dark-colored roses during temperature extremes. You may consider using shade cloths or applying mulch around the base of the plants to regulate soil temperature and prevent heat stress or cold damage.

To further enhance the color intensity of your dark-colored roses, consider providing them with a well-draining soil rich in organic matter. This will help retain moisture while preventing waterlogging, which can lead to root rot. Regular watering is crucial, especially during the warmer months, to keep the soil evenly moist, but not overly saturated.

In conclusion, growing dark-colored roses requires careful consideration of sunlight and temperature. Providing adequate sunlight while protecting the plants from extreme heat is essential for vibrant and healthy blooms. Similarly, maintaining moderate temperatures and ensuring well-draining soil will contribute to the overall success of your dark-colored rose garden. By creating the ideal growing conditions, you can enjoy the beauty and allure of black roses, deep purple varieties, and other dark-colored roses in your garden.

Soil Amendments and Fertilization for Dark-Colored Roses

Dark-colored roses, such as black and deep red varieties, bring a sense of mystery and elegance to any garden. However, these unique blooms require some special care to ensure they reach their full potential. In this subchapter, we will explore soil amendments and fertilization techniques specifically tailored to cultivate dark-colored roses.

When it comes to soil amendments, the key is to create a nutrient-rich and well-draining environment for your roses. Start by preparing the soil before planting your roses. Incorporate organic matter, such as compost or well-rotted manure, to improve the soil structure and enhance its ability to retain moisture. Dark-colored roses tend to have larger, more vibrant blooms when grown in slightly acidic soil with a pH range of 6.0-6.5. You can lower the soil pH by adding elemental sulfur or organic acidifiers.

Fertilization is essential to provide dark-colored roses with the necessary nutrients for healthy growth and abundant blooms. Begin by conducting a soil test to determine the nutrient levels. Based on the results, choose a balanced slow-release fertilizer with a higher phosphorus (P) content. Phosphorus promotes root development and flower production, making it particularly important for dark-colored roses.

Apply the fertilizer in early spring, just as new growth appears, and again in late spring or early summer. Follow the manufacturer's instructions for application rates and techniques. Avoid over-fertilization, as this can lead to excessive foliage growth at the expense of flower production.

To further enhance the color intensity of your dark-colored roses, consider using a fertilizer formulated specifically for roses. These fertilizers often contain additional micronutrients, such as iron and manganese, which can help intensify the pigmentation in the petals.

In addition to soil amendments and fertilization, regular watering is crucial for the health and vitality of dark-colored roses. Water deeply at the base of the plants, rather than overhead, to prevent the foliage from getting wet and minimize the risk of disease.

By following these soil amendments and fertilization techniques, you can ensure that your dark-colored roses thrive and display their unique and enchanting beauty. With proper care, your garden will become a haven for these rare and exotic varieties, creating a stunning display of color and elegance.

Disease and Pest Management for Dark-Colored Roses

When it comes to growing dark-colored roses, such as black roses, there are a few extra considerations to keep in mind. These unique and captivating flowers require special care to maintain their rich hues and prevent diseases and pests from wreaking havoc on their delicate petals. In this subchapter, we will explore the essential disease and pest management techniques that every gardener should know when cultivating dark-colored roses.

One of the most common diseases that affect roses of all colors is black spot. However, dark-colored roses are particularly susceptible to this fungal infection due to their darker foliage. To prevent black spot, it is crucial to maintain good air circulation around the plants by spacing them adequately and pruning any overcrowded branches. Regularly inspect the leaves for early signs of black spot, such as black spots with yellow halos, and promptly remove and destroy any infected foliage. Additionally, avoid overhead watering as this can encourage the spread of the disease. Instead, water the plants at the base to keep the foliage dry.

Another disease that dark-colored roses may be prone to is powdery mildew. This fungal infection appears as a white powdery coating on the leaves and stems. To prevent powdery mildew, provide adequate sunlight and maintain good air circulation around the plants. Remove any infected parts and consider using fungicides if necessary.

In terms of pests, aphids can be a common problem for roses of all colors, including dark-colored varieties. These small insects can cause significant damage by sucking the sap from the leaves and stems. To control aphids, regularly inspect the plants and manually remove them with a strong jet of water or by applying insecticidal soap if the infestation is severe.

Lastly, it is essential to monitor for any signs of other common rose pests, such as thrips, spider mites, and sawflies. These pests can damage the flowers and foliage, leading to a decline in the overall health of the plants. Promptly address any infestations by using appropriate insecticides or implementing natural pest control methods.

By following these disease and pest management techniques, gardeners can ensure that their dark-colored roses remain healthy and vibrant. With proper care, these captivating flowers will continue to enchant and delight with their deep, mysterious hues for years to come.

Preserving the Intensity and Richness of Dark-Colored Roses

Dark-colored roses, such as black and deep red varieties, exude an air of mystery and elegance in any garden. Their intense hues can create a captivating visual impact and become the centerpiece of your rose collection. However, maintaining the vibrancy and richness of dark-colored roses can be a challenge. In this subchapter, we will explore the techniques and tips to ensure your dark-colored roses remain intense and stunning.

First and foremost, it is crucial to select the right variety of dark-colored roses. Not all roses can achieve the desired depth of color, so it is essential to choose varieties specifically bred for their dark hues. Varieties like 'Black Baccara,' 'Mister Lincoln,' and 'Black Magic' are renowned for their intense colors and are ideal choices to begin with.

To preserve the intensity of dark-colored roses, proper sunlight exposure is essential. While roses require at least six hours of direct sunlight, dark-colored varieties prefer slightly less intense sunlight. They can be prone to fading under direct, scorching sunlight, so consider planting them in areas with partial shade or where they receive filtered sunlight during the hottest parts of the day.

Another crucial aspect of maintaining the richness of dark-colored roses is proper watering. Adequate moisture is essential, but overwatering can lead to dilution of the pigments, resulting in a lighter color. Water your roses deeply and infrequently, ensuring the soil is well-drained. Mulching around the base of the plants can help retain moisture and prevent weeds, which compete for water and nutrients.

Regular fertilizing is vital for all roses, but dark-colored varieties benefit from specific nutrient formulations. Look for rose fertilizers with higher potassium content, as it helps enhance flower color and overall plant health. Apply the fertilizer according to the package instructions, usually during the growing season and after each bloom cycle.

Lastly, be mindful of pests and diseases that can affect the health and color of your dark-colored roses. Regularly inspect your plants for common rose ailments like black spot, aphids, and powdery mildew. Promptly treat any issues with appropriate organic or chemical remedies to ensure your roses remain healthy and vibrant.

By following these techniques and tips, you can preserve the intensity and richness of your dark-colored roses. With proper care, these captivating flowers will continue to dazzle and enchant, adding an element of drama and sophistication to your garden.

Conclusion: Celebrating the Diverse Beauty of Roses and Your Journey as a Rose Gardener

Congratulations, fellow rose gardeners! We have reached the end of our journey through the enchanting world of roses. Throughout this book, we have explored the secrets and techniques to successfully grow roses of all colors, including the elusive black roses. We have delved into the art of cultivating vibrant red, pure white, delicate pink, sunny yellow, regal purple, mesmerizing blue, and even multi-colored roses. We have also learned how to care for rare and exotic rose varieties, creating a garden filled with a diverse range of colors that will leave everyone in awe.

As gardeners, we share a passion for the beauty and elegance that roses bring to our lives. Each one has its own personality, its own story to tell. From the velvety petals of the red roses symbolizing love and passion, to the delicate and pure white roses representing innocence and purity, each color holds a special meaning and adds a unique touch to our gardens.

Growing roses of different shades has allowed us to create stunning floral displays that bring joy and tranquility to our outdoor spaces. The vibrant hues of yellow roses have brightened our days, while the enchanting purple roses have added a touch of mystery and royalty. And who can resist the allure of the rare and captivating blue roses? These ethereal blooms have become the centerpiece of our gardens, drawing admiration from all who lay eyes on them.

We have also discovered that cultivating black roses and other dark-colored varieties requires special care and attention. These roses, with their velvety petals and intense hues, demand a unique set of nurturing techniques. From providing them with rich soil and ample sunlight to protecting them from pests and diseases, we have learned to give these dark beauties the love they need to thrive.

Our journey as rose gardeners has been filled with learning, patience, and dedication. We have faced challenges, celebrated successes, and grown alongside our beloved roses. But most importantly, we have learned to appreciate the diverse beauty that these flowers bring into our lives.

So, fellow gardeners, as we conclude this chapter, let us celebrate the diverse beauty of roses and the incredible journey we have embarked upon. May your gardens continue to flourish with roses of all colors, filling your lives with their beauty, fragrance, and symbolism. May your love for these enchanting flowers inspire others to join this wonderful world of rose gardening. And may your journey as a rose gardener be filled with joy, fulfillment, and an everlasting love for these magnificent blooms. Happy gardening!